The Mix Up

~~~

By Laura Bedford

ISBN-13: 978-1463661687
ISBN-10: 1463661681

......This great hologram called Creation...
It's all a cosmic play, and there is nothing but you!

Itzhak Bentov (1923 – 1979)
Scientist, Inventor, Author, Mystic

The Mix Up is dedicated to all children who do not hear nearly often enough of their goodness, their beauty and their value in our world.

Your radiant presence is reminding us what matters most.

Acknowledgements

To the Loving One and everyone along my way.

You never cease to remind me what matters most.

Prologue

The Mix Up is a happy book sharing in joyful ways why it matters to see only the Light, our beauty and radiance, and how only mind, human ideas of guilt, fear, shame, blame and suffering paralyze the human heart. By our very nature, we contain and are immersed within higher intelligence that offers easy solutions to all our woes. The Mix Up is all about strengthening our willingness to trust our heart, our still center, intuition—how we access Divine intelligence—so heaven on earth becomes a moment-to-moment experience for children, for adults and for the earth and all who journey here. As we recognize the wholeness of Life, we transform.

My family lost a three-month old baby name Michael when my older brother was seven and I was five. Michael's death, perhaps more than any other single event, informed the dynamics of our family unit. After his death, I worried and cried myself to sleep for years afraid I would lose my parents and my older brother. We visited Michael's grave on Sundays, after church. Images of my brother and myself gazing lovingly upon our baby brother were etched onto his headstone. Soon, a new baby brother and sister came along, and life moved on. Through the years my perplexity about this thing called Life ignited. As a felt sense, I began to wonder, "Why does suffering exist? It doesn't seem right." And, "Why can't I remember where I come from?" You know, before being born.

As a child I saw the sky as pink, not as blue, all day every day. One day, in an instant in my perception, it turned to blue. Asking around, I discovered that no one, at least in my world, had been seeing a pink sky. Thankfully, nothing else turned from pink to blue or seemed to change in any way. For the first time it dawned on me viscerally that "I" was in a very strange place. Truly, the sky changing color was not nearly so disorienting (this kid loves wild stuff) as the death of my baby brother and realizing that no one had been seeing a pink sky. What else wasn't quite right?

I recognized from an early age that it is important trust our inner knowing because not everyone else does, and to honor feelings and let go of guilt and fear. It would take decades and lots of suffering experiences—not trusting my heart—before I realized why it matters so much. As you read The Mix Up, I pray you trust your own heart's song and your own feeling sense, allowing all less than peaceful thoughts and states-of-being to dissolve. The only "thing" that stops our flow, our Life, is fear and feeling guilty for trusting our heart's song. As our ego dissolves and Light is more deeply felt, the belief that we are separate and guilty of only ego knows what, we wake up to what has always been.

You are a miracle.

You are everything.

To remember, enter.

What We Need

Our Life provides exactly what we need to wake up to the Truth that only Love is real.

Only Love is Real

Humanity is on a cosmic mission of extraordinary significance.
We are fully prepared for the adventure of the sage. As our most
cherished teachers of peace have always shared, we have forever
been safely held in Love, in the Light of perfect peace.
Only our mind, our human perception, is slightly mixed up regarding our unity and
the astonishing splendor of who we really are and where we really are (in Heaven).

Adventure within The Mix Up to experience your radiant Light in ways you
may not have ever imagined. Then share your delight with children who
are not hearing often enough of their own radiant Light, their beauty,
their value and their gifts for a world that seems fear-less than perfect.
We are the Light of the world every time we trust our bright heart.

What is our Light? Our Light is our Love. Our Light is our joy and our heart's song.
Our Light is that which overlooks the errors of this world, our own and another's.

As we trust our Light and the Light within all Life, and, as we overlook the seeming
mistakes and misperceptions of this world, we help others, especially children, to
remember their own Light and, together, we waken to the Heaven we never left.

In practical ways, The Mix Up transports us beyond form, space and time. In the spirit
of the greatest adventure stories ever told, we are here
to complete a journey begun eons ago that—get this—
according to Jesus and others never really took place![1]

Our expedition orders may seem tall, but they are really very small.

Here they stand:

---

1 Enlightened beings, including Jesus in the *Bible, A Course in Miracles* and other scripture, are clear
that this world is a dream, an illusion. Our mind is caught in its own matrix of fear. Jesus and others
transcended fear and guilt in the mind. They share how to do this quickly by trusting Love and Light.
There is only One Mind. When we wake up we realize we never left our Light/Heaven where we are
aware of what we are.

Trust your joy and the Light of All.
Forgive the whole world. The world is an illusion.
Release fear. Let go of guilt and blame.
Listen within the stillness of your heart.[2]

Focus on Love and Light

No matter any mind's story, focus on Love and Light in you and in all.

*Follow your own heart's joy and innocence
with glee, and support others to do the same.
What do YOU love? What brings you to LIFE?*

Why is this vital for awakening to the Heaven we never left?

*We are One, yet this is hard to realize if we are not honoring our Soul's song.
We do not vibrate highly and smoothly if we follow a "wrong for us" song.*

*And, it is more of an adventure to overlook all error
when we are not loving and trusting our own heart.*

*It is easy to overlook error when we value our own heart's song because we see that
others deserve to follow their heart's song as well. A happy, joyful flow of Life ensues.*

You are Light.

The Illumined Master Jeshua/Jesus explains with clarity,

*"Grace is your natural state. When you are not in a state of grace,
you are out of your natural environment and do not function well.[3]"*

When you do not feel like you are functioning well, or that another is not...

*Go within, beyond any notion or potion of doubt.
Encourage another to trust the Light within all.
Divine Intelligences knows exactly how to be.*

*We are all this Light encompassing all, but we
do not perceive the real Heaven we are in.[4]*

---

3 *A Course in Miracles*
4 Jesus and many others are clear that this world is *not* Heaven. We are always immersed within Heaven, the Great Rays and eternal peace and joy beyond imagining, however, we do not yet perceive this.

Thoughts Results are Simultaneous

Cause and effect are instant.

Remember, as long proved...

Time is taking place at ONE.

Be heart-full with thinking.

Trust only thoughts of Light.

~ ~ ~

The thought is upon us...

Theo is ultimate science.

Now

*In any moment, you can remember
what and where you really are.*

Reach gently within.

Never force.

Always Still.

Trust the inner smile.

If your heart resists, persist.

(You are not a victim. You are Light.)

Note about the World

We appear to live in a world both beautiful and horrific.

Hearts defend and leap in joy in the same moment.

We have already the key to knowing why inside.

We have forgotten where we really are.

To remember, enter Heart stillness.

~ ~ ~

Trust the radiance of the Inner Light. Always.

You are not alone. You are never alone.

Just like Neo, you are The One.[5]

Don't trust sad or mad. Trust the Light.

Trust the miracle of Unconditional Love.

Look beyond any shadows in your mind.

~ ~ ~

Only Love and Light is real.

---

5   Neo is a character from the1999 film *The Matrix*.

Welcome Into The Mix Up!

The Mix Up is a book to heal wary hearts. Ignite your Inner
Light and the Inner Light of children encountered along your
way. Connect through your heart's Light intention.

Journey within your experience! Feel what it is like to **be** Your Fully Radiant Light.

A few definitions for common words appear within The Mix Up.

These definitions are meant only as awareness expanders.

If you wonder what feels right for you, ask your heart.

~ ~ ~

Helpful bits as you begin to adventure within...

Divine Intelligence trusts that, within stillness, all that is needed arises.

If a moment feels blue, remember Light's helpful glue.

There is only Love or a call for Love.
A Course in Miracles

Our Golden Sun Bow Sphere

You are and you are bathed in Golden Sun Bow Light. Always.

*When atmospheric conditions are aligned in a
particular way those who gaze see what is always here.*

*Meditate on your Sacred Heart and the Golden Sun Bow Sphere of You.
Imagine your Golden Sun Bow Sphere expanding to infinity inward and out.
Let go into the Love inside of you. If your mind resists, send it Love and Light.*

Return to this heart and perception healing practice as often as you like.

Connect with the Inner Light

Our journey will be revealing in a loving you way! Consider the following:
We know that to unmix our thoughts and connect with our Inner Light
(God/Divine Intelligence/happiness/peace/joy/love/kindness/abundance)
an inner shift into peaceful awareness, beyond all thought, is necessary.

To make a genuine shift, will yourself to release thought-forms of judgment,
shame and blame of self or others, the only "thinks" that keep peace away.
As we move into our heart space we dissolve upset and transcend our fear.
As we trust Love rather than our fear of Love (ego) our Radiant Light shines.
We are clearer receivers of Divine Intelligence/Source-thoughts, the One.

Peace and joy is always present. Now. This moment. Can you feel it?
The core of your Still Being always knows peace, joy and happiness.

At any age, making the Inner Shift is actually quite easy and natural.
(Trusting Love is an astounding and miraculous adventure for all of us!)

The Mix Up explores why it matters to offer our willingness to shift.
(Hint: We restore our awareness of what and where we really are.)

Our ego will always object to trusting Light when we are upset.
Yet, we are simply surrendering our attachment to what is false.
To restore reality to awareness, let go into the Love inside you.

*Don't think. **Be** (aware). Trust your joy and Light, not shadow.*

If you are a skeptic, I promise, if you journey, you will discover something great inside.
The Mix Up is for those who wish to end suffering for self, others and the world. It may
be especially useful for those working with children and our own radiant inner child.

For those inclined to the pessimist inside,

or who are plain wary to the bone,

let go of the onerous and glide!

Together, we're in for a ONEdrous ride!

Stop, Look In, Listen

Have you ever felt less than?

Don't sweat the cause.

Trust the Inner Pause.

~ ~ ~

Our mind is veiled to the Light.

Go within your heart.

You are Cherished Beyond Measure

You are SO worth it!

Does this sound right?

You are Oh So Loved!

Call on the Light Within if you forget.

Ask to Know the Truth.

Know that you are worthy.
(And so is everyONE else.)

Relax deeply within your heart.

To our ego, this may sound impractical to downright wrong, but remember, our mind is veiled to wonder. Can we respond to life in a more helpful and fulfilling way if we are wracked with concerns and guilt or focusing on dislike? We obsess over the silly. Some die or kill for it. Look to your heart. Significantly, we are not to judge our past judgments. We are to forgive. Look within to recognize the incredible Light that lives within us all.

Join together. Radiantly love us. We are absolutely great.

Remember your gifts. Encourage others to remember theirs.

Everything is Love

When you feel the urge to judge,
give your heart a gentle nudge.

Hear the call for Love.

Love Is

Love is the only creative Source in existence.

You have never been anything but Love and Light.

Wake to Your Inner Light

It's easy. Trust the Light in all Life.

You are the Universal Light Source.

Dance the universal night away.

You are a portal of possibility.

Trust the stillness of Now.

A Young Man Chooses the Inner Path

Many years ago I lived at a yoga retreat center.

Yoga means "union with the Divine."

Absolutely Divine is what we are.

During my stay, I learned the story of a young man who also lived there.

He was not much older than perhaps twenty-three.
He told me he had great challenges focusing in school.
His mind would wander. It just wasn't much fun.
Doctors wanted to put him on medication.

He said, "No, thank you."

He had learned of yoga and enlightened beings.

He wanted to try the Inner Journey instead.

His mother agreed. So, he did.

He liked what he found within.

He was a gentle creature.

A helpful, kind friend.

Trust your Inner Light.

Those with highly sensitive minds (and nervous systems) can undertake many practices to find the Inner Light. As we do, we unearth astounding information that has always been written within us. Always trust your inner guide, your intuition, to lead you to helpful teachings and temporary teachers. Put your faith in you and in the Light, and trust that all are Light. We know innately when we are listening to our Light or to ego's unpeace.

Going within naturally helps calm the ego. Assuring grown-ups and kids they are amazing calms the ego/fear-mind and nervous system. The Inner Light is real.

Depression

Depression is among the leading causes of death in our western world.

Are we okay with this?

We have forgotten the wisdom to slow and go within. Depression is a gift.

When we do not support our Light, our heart's song, we suffer.

Our physiology begins to mirror our collective internal state.

Trust that you are worth honoring first.

Not with arrogance, but with Light.

Trust that others are worth honoring.

Peace and joy comes from within.

Give peace "a change"

of your heart and mind.

Ask for help from those who understand Light.

Celebrate Life!

Release your worry.

You are Light!

Nothing needs to be different.

Ask the angels to help if you blurry.

The Great Inner Awakening

*We are living within an auspicious era, an era that has been foretold
as a great awakening, a unified shift in awareness, an Age of Light.*

*The Age of Light is within us. When we remember Love we are dissolving an ancient
mix up in our mind about who and where we really are. Our existential fear is being
unearthed. Misperception is being brought to Light so it may be dissolved forever.*

*We are learning, as the awake have always shared, we never really left Heaven.
Evidence for our mind's radiant awakening is written everywhere, in our sacred
teachings, within the cosmos, within our heart and within the hearts of children.*

Shift is in the air. We all feel a higher purpose within our very wave~particles.

*Our broken hearts are opening because we are asking them to open. We
are less willing to trust stories of hate and thoughts of upset and division that
keep humanity in a "middle," a half thriving, half broken existence. We are
reaching in heartfully. We are journeying inside asking for better information
and for our Light to shine. We are allowing ourselves to feel Love no matter
what pesky stories our ego strives to perpetuate. Our willing heart is drawing
us closer together and closer to awakening to the revelation that we are a
single sacred being, a unity that only appears to be less than whole. We are
remembering that our heart is aware of something much grander than what we
call "the little self." We are recognizing that only Love is real. The other side of
the veil, where we "go" when we "die" is right here, right now. Peace is here.*

*The mix up into fear, shame and blame is temporary.
All we need is to forgive this world.
If this sounds like a tall order, never worry. All is Love.
Go within. Ask to know what is real.*

*We are eternal radiant Light. As we are willing our heart to face the
shadow in our mind that loves to attract to itself to the strange and
wary, we are facilitating our awakening. As we face the illusory dark
and transcend it, we enlighten to the remembrance of what is always
true: Love's Light. We realize we never left Heaven's embrace. We are safe.*

In our age of technological enlightenment, the light bulb is going on. Yet, our little self goes on about trying to convince itself of imperfection and impurity, wanting more of what never leads to anything but a cycle of missing everything that matters. When we begin to remember that, as One, we have everything we could possibly need and that nothing outside of us satisfies for eternity, the Light heart in us begins the journey within. We begin to trust. Our Inner Light wakes each of us peacefully in the perfect moment.

Enjoy!

Be still.

Open your heart.

Ask to know.

In Joy your Light.

All that is not joy is a dream.

Thoughts that Block Light

The Mix Up is about gently releasing thoughts that block the Light of who we really are and where we really are. As you adventure within be a witness to yourself. As you witness your own Light, you help children and adults to do the same.

Thought knowledge has been shared throughout history by our esteemed teachers of unconditional Love and peace. It is known within our heart.

The Mix Up is a self-nourishing adventure into what is true in you.

Fly lightly inward toward your boundless radiant bliss.

Start at the start or journey with random delight.

Travel into your experience. Trust your intuition.

Enjoy whatever experience you are having.
Relish the awareness of your subtle sense.

If this feels a little weird at first, great!
Trust only your peaceful sensations,
yet allow all sensation to be a-okay.

A journey of this nature, taken this day,
will reveal your own Radiant Inner Light!

Each page weaves a radiant key to your Golden Holy Grail.
Your heart will guide perfectly for how to proceed on the trail.

Merrily, trust the inside sense to guide and give bearings.
Savor that which evokes the Inspirited Light Heart in you.

Remember to share your feelings with the Light and
with others who can hear your heart and who trust
your Light goodness when you do not remember.

Set an Intention to Release Upset

For optimal effect reading The Mix Up,

establish an intention for a new awareness.

Bring into your heart something that is upsetting.

Allow the idea to gently float into your awareness.

Be sure not to judge yourself or the circumstance.

Now bless your heart and this thorny situation.

Take a deep, cleansing breath and let go.

There is no need to understand or to

analyze. Always trust Love to lead.

The journey is about connecting with and releasing our radiant Inner Light.
Turn gently inward to Love to face what blocks Light from your awareness.

As we take care of each other, we release everyone from an ancient guilt.
Remember, even if unthinkable to concede, everything is always truly One.

Be aware, our ego might think we don't feel our unity, yet we always do.
When we trust Love we instantly set us all free, beyond space-time of 4D.

Real peace and joy may seem unfamiliar in our present world circumstance.
Yet, on an existential level, we know the wary and the strange is not just right.

Our Inner Light will guide for how to be true and lovingly kind.

As we trust, we help children to center within their heart's Light core.

Note: Inner Light is the same as Christ Light/God-realization. Jesus
was a being that transcended fear and guilt within His mind, which
caused Inner Light Realization. He is teaching us how to do this
by overlooking all error and seeing all Life as Divine Light.

A Cosmic Mission

Trust your cosmic mission into the Great Light of You.

You are fully prepared for the adventure of the sages.

We are safely held in gentle Love.

~ ~ ~

To awaken, Love all Life mightily.

Release all dreams this night.

Awaken to your Inner Light.

(There is no need to rush the Light.
Always trust everything is all right.)

Mission Specialists

Life/Divine Intelligence gives us exactly what we ask for.

Words are not prayer.

Vibes are prayer.

To awaken, be aware.

What are you really asking for?

Never fear fear. Offer fear to the Light.

~ ~ ~

Divine Intelligence knows Love's vibe.

Let Love soothe.

Trust the in joy vibe.

Trust the inner peace vibe.

When We Trust Fear

When we trust fear and upset to guide,

fear and upset manifests in the world.

Trust Love to guide.

Definitions for Adventurers

Definitions for key words follow below. As you journey translate words into vocabulary that feels comfortable for you. In a mission of this nature, it is always an adventure to choose language. Look to how much our mind fights or rages over a particular word. Language can lead to war or peace. When we all sit down and listen with heart, we'll wake up to reality—to the Heaven we never left—really, really, really, really, fast!

Our purpose is to end pain and suffering by awakening to our Radiant Light. This Light is real. Once we have accessed it fully, it never leaves us again.

Our heart knows to forgive what feels wrong and to look within. Ask your heart for the intention behind all words. Feel for Love.

Intention is frequency. Vibe creates. Trust Love-word vibes.

~ ~ ~

Key Mission Definitions for Love and Light Scientists

Divine Intelligence/God/the Absolute/Light/One Spirit/Our True Nature
Divine Intelligence/One/All That Is/Being/Infinite/Beyond Imagining
Divine Intelligence is Absolute Awareness of Truth/Omnipotent
Divine Intelligence knows beyond human ideas/paradigms
Divine Intelligence is innately loving, peaceful, coherent, joyful
Only Love/Divine Intelligence/God/Absolute Awareness is real

Ego = Fear/Sense of Separation/Amnesia of Oneness/Lack/Blame/ Sense of Brokenness/Aloneness/Shame/Guilt/Lack of Peace/Attack
Ego/fear/aloneness/separation is not real. We are safely held in Love always. Ego encourages us to be sad or mad. Our ego and perceived lack of safety feels very real as we identify with the body. Ego is an idea of "me" at the expense of "we." The "me" is fine, except when the "me" forgets the "we," which blocks awareness of the Light. Ego fears Oneness/Unity, yet this is nothing to fear. Ego will present as any experience that feels upsetting or energetically dissonant. What does not feel peaceful, joyful or safe (i.e., held in Light) is **an experience**

not to be admonished if we wish to dissolve it. Here's why: Admonishing scares ego and disregards our purpose for being here. Ego/fear exists only within a mind that is dreaming of what it is not. Belief in fear and unOneness veils our Light, the recollection of what and where we really are. No one is worth less. During an ego upset say, "It's okay. Never fear. I am Light unrecognized."

Defining Fear

Let's look closely at how the word "fear" is being used within The Mix Up by first exploring **what fear is not**. We do not speak of awareness for the physical world. Being aware of our form's relativity and dimension is helpful as it helps keeps our physical bodies safe as much as possible. All form eventually shifts back into Light. As we honor form, we tune into the flow of Divine Intelligence for how to care for it.

The fear The Mix Up refers to is an **inner felt sense of resistance** to "what is" right now. When we are not happy, we have made a choice to experience what we are not.[6] Allowing the flow of Light through us helps dissolve fear, i.e., all energetic dissonance. The energy of our fear is not real. It is blocked frequency that simply needs space to smooth. Yet, fear (upset/any unpeaceful state) feels profoundly fearful and real to us when we're in the midst. When we resist (fight or deny) our energetic experience, we deny our Light's right to exist, to experience **the absence** of Light. This is our wish.[7]

Confusion comes into our mind when it begins making up stories or feeding stories. Since some, or many, moments can feel quite strange to downright horrific, from our perspective (anger, frustration, depression, aloneness, irritation, grief, jealousy, feeling less than/lack of self-Love or blaming others, all unpeaceful states), this awareness may take some getting used to. However, when we honor—don't resist—a felt sense of fear regarding a perceived lack of joy or peace, we will become aware of an inner shift.

The inner shift is a felt experience of Inner Light. Are we paying attention to it?

So, fear is actually hinting us toward our Light! Great Light is found within! (Bring to heart how enlightened beings are peaceful in terrible moments.)

Fear is a prompt within us to shift our focus to the inkling of our Light. While paradoxical to our ego, this allows fear to dissolve naturally.

---

6   Holy Spirit's Interpretation of the New Testament, and many teachings speak well of this Soul choice.
7   See The Mix Up page called "A Spark of Light Split" or refer to A Course in Miracles or any teaching of Jesus' regarding how our Light/Mind "separated" or "split" from God/Divine Intelligence/Our True Nature. The split/separation never actually occurred. Our awareness of Divine Intelligence/God is merely veiled.

Inner~restingly, no one can undo fear for us, except us!
Not even an enlightened being! We are truly free Light.

As fear dissolves, our connection with Divine Intelligence is re-Cognized.

Rocket to the Center of Your Heart

*We are moving at the speed of thought. Our ego mind's thought is slow and dense.
We are moving at God-speed, at the speed of Divine Intelligence, at the speed
of super-consciousness being, far beyond what our human mind believes is Light.*

*Our mind must rest to attune to God-speed, which is the same as stillness.
Trust your subtle felt sense. Truth lies beyond energy-in-motion (emotion).*

*Rocket gently beyond clouds of doubt, the tiny
shadow of fear and drear. You are not your fear.*

*Relax ego's resistance to the Bright Light of Inner Play.
Do not be concerned for past or future. Trust the now.*

*Your heart's awareness is thousands of times
more powerful than your mind's awareness.*

*If you find yourself not believing in your heart's power,
in the power of simply relaxing into subtle awareness,
never fear. Be aware of what you feel. Subtle Light.*

Pay attention to what is occurring within your field.

*If you find your mind perpetuating a story of shame
or blame, it is challenging to sense subtle frequencies.*

Ask yourself how you feel when you are in a story of pain.

Pay attention to this felt sense and then relax more deeply.

Expand into the super-conscious You that knows it is whole.

Suffering ceases the moment we trust Love.

Thoughts are Geometry

Trust only Lovingkind thoughts and feeeelings.

Let go of all unkind thoughts from anyone.

Why?

*All thoughts are geometry. They create our experience.
Love's Light is always present beyond all thought forms.*[8]

As often as you can, transcend thought forms.

Really?

Yup.

*Imagine, next time you are thinking, the shape of your thoughts.
Bring into your awareness how your thoughts feel.
What do they look like? What color are they?*

0000000000 ~ imagine a circular, oval or cloud shape to thought-forms.

As we alert ourselves to unfun thoughts, we are empowered to shift.

Shifting into stillness is essential to undoing unkindness in the world.

(It helps to remember that all that is not peace is a call for Love.)

If doubt rises within, remember the angels!

Remember, you are never, ever alone.

Ask for help from your One Love team.

---

8   Mind creates. Mind never sleeps. Thought-forms are mental energy/geometry. Feelings-forms are emotional energy/geometry. Deeply felt thoughts are naturally creative. Focus on stillness and witness.

Light and Thought

Our mind's thoughts are dense, slow moving Light. (Divine thought is still.)
For a fun experiment, adventure by observing Light refracting in water.

Light bends (refracts) when it enters the substance of water.

When observing from the surface, an object
below the water is not where it appears to be.

Experiment by placing a long skinny object into a glass of water so that part of the
object remains above the surface and part of the object lies below the surface.

Notice the location of the portion of the object that remains above the surface.
Notice the apparent location of the portion of the object below the surface.

Does the object above the surface align
directly with itself below the surface?

Hold this observation in your heart as you ponder your own
thoughts leaving your mind and traveling through space-time.

When we think, our thought-energy travels instantly and refracts in space-time.

Split-mind thought extends and bends the plasma of space-time making illusion.
Divine thoughts hold and pass through the plasma of space-time. They are real.

Now transcend your thoughts. Let go softly into stillness.
Does this seem easier said than done? Trust your practice.
Now is the only moment it is possible to align beyond time.

Our True Loving Nature knows exactly where we are.

~ ~ ~

For those who Love the science of Divine Intelligence, our
mind will come to discover far more about anti-matter, dark
matter and dark energy from a place of stillness.
Hold a desire to know within your being and transcend your thoughts into stillness.

Thought and Energy

All thought, all deeply held belief, is energy.
Energy tends to follow the path of resistance. What?!

In the illusion, what you trust (Love or the
absence of Love) is what you experience.

This is why we will often see minds gather under the banner of a particular belief/
thought-system and why it can feel challenging to "let go" of an experience
that is clearly not joyful or peaceful, but that also feels too
fearful to leave. Ego will call this zone "safety" because it fears
the unknown, even though we are not feeling safe.

Indeed, we are far more comfortable with systems that support fear's existence.

The mind will resist Love until it feels safe enough or weary enough to seek within.

In effect, the most important journey is the inner journey to our Light.
Yet, we will not find the Inner Light by cycling stories of shame or pain.

Become aware of your thoughts. Become aware of what you focus on.
For a few moments each day attempt to transcend thought altogether.
Entering stillness may seem anywhere from uncomfortable to impossible.
Yet, You already know how. Activate your Golden Sun Bow Sphere.

Masters are clear that an untrained mind can accomplish nothing.
Mind is alive. Form comes after mind. Form follows consciousness.

Next time you are thinking, witness the energetic flow. Notice how you feel inside.

Bring to heart stories that convey a master teacher (an enlightened being) working
with an adept. Often the student will be given mundane tasks like floor scrubbing,
bathroom cleaning, tasks that will push an ego's resistance and fears to the surface.
Ego often lashes out at the teacher as being the cause of the suffering that the
ego is experiencing. This gives the master and the student a place to begin.

Thought-suffering, i.e, judging our experience of Life, is
always optional. Fear is always optional. Life is never dull.
Deep insight will come while conducting mundane tasks.

Heart Resonating Awareness

*Several key awareness' speed our awakening. It helps
profoundly to activate our heart's magnetic field to assist us.
Also, it is helpful to give our mind (ego) something to do, to focus
upon. Some use mantra, any phrase that helps calm our nervous system.
You can make up your own mantra or find one that feels lovely and calming.
Or, focus your attention on a candle flame, a plant, a flower, anything beautiful.*

*Our physical heart's field/crystalline magnet is measured as 5,000 times more
powerful than our brain's field.[9] When we intentionally activate our heart's field,
we are facilitating a transcendent state. This is super wondrously Light powerful.*

All adventurers, be sure to activate your heart's happy magnetic field often!

*Vibrate and oscillate with Love's gratitude.
You may find yourself seeing the Great Rays!*

*To activate your heart's core, bring to awareness a thought that is lovely.
Ponder your appreciation for Love itself, for your laughter or another's,
for a beautiful sunrise or sunset, or a thunderstorm, or crystalline flakes
of snow, for the smile of an infant, for your willingness to explore the
sparkle of your wondrous nature when you're sad or mad.*

Imagine your inner beauty as a radiant sun bow!

Relax into your sparkling Light oscillations.

Trust your waving heart to guide you.

Even if you feel especially ridiculous!

---

9   Research by scientists working with the Institute of Heartmath, heartmath.org

Effortless Shifting

It takes no energy to shift into our
natural state as Divine Intelligence.

In our state, we are used to efforting.

Choosing suffering is a choice. It wastes.

Say to that pesky downward spiral,
"Oh, goodness me. Let's go up!"

Relax. Feel the inner wind.

Go within to Love.

Humanity's Split-Mind

*Ask yourself who you truly are and where you
came from before you were born into a body.*

Be not concerned if nothing seems to happen, though it might!

*Since ancient times it has been shared that our mind is veiled or split
from the awareness of who we really are and where we really are.*

(Bring to mind our long held belief in death.)

*We are partially unconscious to most of
what is going on within and around us.*

*Our primary difficulty is that we have forgotten that we are fundamentally One, a
unified consciousness, a singularity of awareness that has temporarily taken form.
Our ego was "born" as our amnesia became more acute, and this
ego blocks the awareness of who and where we really are. Bring
to mind the ancient quest for Truth, the search for enlightenment,
our fascination with discovery and striving for peace.*

*We need only look within and around to observe how our amnesia
of our origin, our split-minded state, has us forgetting Love. As we
remember Love, the split in our mind heals. Our continued disregard
for Life leads to horrific internal and external suffering.*

Removing our focus from upsetting stories and Loving dissolves our upsets.

*Much of humanity continues to project inwardly and outwardly
due to this deep confusion within the psyche. Our upsets are
actually quite easily dissolved with a few key understandings. All
enlightened beings encourage us to look within for peace.*

We are all familiar with the Golden Rule, the guidance to see only the Light.

The inner journey, and caring for each other always, wakes us up quickly.

Let go into every Inner Light revealing experience. Giggle and whirl!

*We'll begin straight away on the next
page helping the whole of the world!*

The Golden Sun Bow Sphere

Imagine all children in the world within a Golden Sun Bow Sphere.

*(If desired, return to the Golden Sun Bow Sphere
meditation near the beginning of The Mix Up.)*

Remain with this vision as long as your heart desires.

Imagine all adults in the world within a Golden Sun Bow Sphere.

Remain with this vision as long as your heart desires.

Imagine all animals in the world within a Golden Sun Bow Sphere.

Remain with this vision for as long as your heart desires.

Imagine the whole world within a Golden Sun Bow Sphere.

If you haven't already, merge the spheres into One.

Say the following deep within your heart.

"You are perfect as you are.

I am perfect as I am.

All misperceptions were long ago forgiven.

Thank you for your gifts and for your Light.

Thank you for existing and for journeying with me."

Remain in a quiet inner space until you feel complete.

On Letting Go

As we move along,

remember where you belong.

In happiness.

In peace.

In joy.

When your mind wants to hang on to story…

Here's the thing. Let go.

When your mind wants to hang on to a person…

Here's the thing. Let go.

We are safely held in happiness.

We are safely held in peace.

We are safely held in joy.

We won't know

until we

let go.

Never fear, this does not mean we depart from what feels perfect and right or a little wrong in our world. We are merely to Love and let go within the mighty Light inside.

A deeply felt sense of Love will guide.

What is for us comes to us naturally.

Good Questions Our Heart Answers Freely

Why do we seem to forget about Love when we are upset?

How come we do not seem to remember Divine Intelligence?

How come we do not seem to remember where we come from?

How come when upset arises we tend to move toward an even more fearful state?

Why do we fear holding children and telling them they are good and beautiful?

Why is it so easy to walk away from that which we do not want to face fully?

Why does ego seem to need to break everyone down before building up?

What happens if we choose to not believe thoughts that are not very kind?

Go inside your heart. Ask about this.

Communication

Communication heals.

If you find yourself wishing for happiness, ask your heart for wisdom.

Do you trust your heart's song?

What brings you happiness and joy?

Are you Lightly supporting the peace and joy of all?

Are you asking another to give up their heart's song for you?

Does it feel like another is asking you to give up your heart's song?

Remember, no one remembers who we are and how we got here.

We're all a little wacky when it comes to feeling safe and secure.

Communicate gently with all beings, in silence and with words.

If another's heart does not connect with yours, it is fine to walk away.

Trust the might of the Inner Light to guide. You deserve to feel great.

Everyone deserves to feel great. No one is outside of the Light.

As long as we trust the Love inside all, we cannot make a mistake.

Heaven and Hell

In our earthly lives, one person's heaven is another person's hell.

Our split-mind is always wanting, striving to manifest, thinking...

"My heaven will be when I have thus and so..."

When we wake up we realize hell never was.

When you find yourself where you do not believe you "want" to be,

gently surrender within. Ask to be shown any judging thoughts.

Allow any sensations behind word-thoughts to float up to see.

Let sensations and thoughts be set free into coheren "see."[10]

Divine Intelligence places us in the perfect circumstances.

Enter gentle stillness. No effort is required.
(And, it can "still" be very loud outside.)

Trust your heart's song.

Forgive all that seems "wrong."

Love with all your might.

Remind your heart, "I am always Light and free."

---

10   As we allow our felt sense to enliven, subtle sensations will become more obvious to us. This is huge and powerful for expanding our awareness. Share all uncomfortable feelings/sensations with the Light. They will smooth out/become coherent. Our form may attune to a sine wave. We are attuning to the Inner Light.

Remember Thrice

All Life is One Radiant Unified Source Field.

All Life is One Radiant Unified Source Field.

All Life is One Radiant Unified Source Field.

We need not believe.

Enter stillness.

Ask To Know.

Go to straight to your Still Radiant Core.

We work miracles when we trust the Light.

The Loopy Hoops

When you find your mind in a loopy hoop (of suffering),

spinning round and round a story of feeling some pain,

release your awareness from the goop of inner poop.

(Even if you think you are alone in
the pain, everyone is feeling it.)

We share the same mind.

Attune to your heart.

This is really quite smart.

Your Inner Being will return to its natural peace.

Soul Light and Higher Awareness

Our Soul Light extends far beyond our physical form.

Our Soul Light is always peaceful. Research this if you wonder.

As you explore, ask for your Soul to become coherent and joyful.

We simply cannot transcend to higher awareness in a state of unrest.

As we focus on joy, we know joy.

As we focus on peace, we know peace.

When we focus on unconditional Loving, we know Love.

When we focus on the opposite of these, guess what...

Assume Our Perfection

A radiant key to awakening...

Always assume perfection and Light.

Do not trust any contrary story in your mind.

Let contrary stories float by and dissolve.

Never judge the tall tale or the teller.

Always assume his/her perfection.

Benefit of the Doubt

Be sure to offer all the benefit of the doubt.

This is how we come to know Love is true.

Judge not another's path or yours.

Our miracles arrive naturally.

Remember thusly,

we are One.

within the All.

Our heart feels this.

What Are You *Feeling*?

It is vital to recognize THAT we are feeling within.

*Swirling Mind and Absolute Awareness of Peace
are two completely independent states of being.*

Where are you in this moment? At heart or in mind?

Only Absolute Awareness of our Heart's Peace is real.

*When we let go into the Light, we always find peace.
Our internal compass is always magnetically aligning
with the inner awareness that feels most safe. Love.*

*When we are feeling our Inner Light, we are
peaceful, and collaborating comes easy.*

Significant Clarifications on Jesus' Teachings

In Jesus' Aramaic "sin" translates as "separate." Wholiness!

He was/is sharing that separation is an illusion. There is only One.

There are many words in sacred writing that require some understanding.

To help speed our awakening (also called quickening or enlightenment, etc.), Jesus shared the Golden Rule to see all Life as sacred and unified in our heart.

It is when our mind forgot/became unconscious of unity that suffering arose.

Not seeing all Life as beautiful, whole Light causes confusion in the mind.

Like Buddha before, to enlighten, to teach and, ultimately, to transcend…

Light dissolved all illusions of guilt, fear, shame and blame in Jesus' mind.

The Inner Light is the same as the Christ Light or Christed Awareness.

Divine Intelligence is All That Is. Love is everything. Even upsets.

This is the awareness realized by Enlightened Masters the world over.

Enlightening is the act of surrendering illusions/fear in our own mind.

No one can do this for us because we are free to believe in illusions.

See our holy adventure and our horror? Horror is self-made.

Though it is taking our mind awhile to understand,

*by the Light! … **now** we've almost got it!*

Mission soon to be accomplished!

A Bit More on the Unreal "Ego" or "Unremembered One"

Everyone born into this blue world has a partly veiled memory.
We do not seem to remember who we are and how we got here.

Some of the time we may not notice or think about
such things, but many of us think about this a lot,
especially those of us who experience the mystical.

Many of us believe we are a body rather than consciousness or mind.
In fact, we are consciousness/mind rather than body. This is important.
Beyond mind-body/consciousness is Pure Awareness. Absolute Knowing.
$$E = mc^2$$
Form is energy that vibrates two times slower than the speed of Light.
This is why we sometimes feel stuck. We are Light, just vibrating slowly.

Love is original. Consciousness is derivative. Both come before form.
Body is a temporary inter-dimensional vehicle, a tool for consciousness.
Body serves. It communicates either Love or fear in any given moment.

Legions throughout history have had mystical experiences that have been
shared in many different ways throughout time. This can be researched.

When we begin to contemplate that we are consciousness rather than body,
we begin to recognize that we have power over our mind/consciousness.
We realize that we are not our upsets nor are we anyone else's upsets.
We are a consciousness that is extremely capable and powerful.
The greatest of our spiritual teachers, Enlightened Masters,
share that we must always go within the Self for better
information. We must pray and meditate and ask
really good questions of our Self and of Love.
Then, we must listen. We must trust that
we cannot change our circumstances
without changing our awareness.
We are a unified consciousness.

Bring to mind the ancient quest for eternal life, enlightenment, awakening,
the holy grail, the search for Truth. These are all the same journey to the same
(w)holy destination we never really left. When we leave the body, we see.

Mission Number One – Explore Your Ego

To begin, start where you are. Simply notice when you feel anything at all.
Trust your felt sense rather than what your mind is telling you to think.
If you feel an upset of any sort, allow it to be okay without judgment.
Feel the sensation and dismiss any thoughts that come up around
why you are upset. In other words, don't take your mind or
anyone else's thoughts and judgments of you personally.
Move beyond the upset. It will dissolve naturally.
Allow your heart to open to the upset for
it to dissolve before taking any action.

If you might, record your blight.

How does the upset feel?

Do not fear fear.

Take notice.

When you're feeling not quite right, ask to know the Light.

Enjoy the weird sensation. Allow it to be all right.

Go deep inside. Trust the flow of Light.

Without doubt, it will smooth out.

Helping Children Help Us Trust the Light

With our memory partly veiled, we do not consciously recall our origin.
Human birth is when our memory becomes veiled to our radiant Light.
Watch a babe and observe when they feel at peace and when in fear.

So too...

Babies may see with the inner I far more clearly than grown-up humans.
Our inner "I" projector rests in the middle of our heart. It attunes to Light.
Kids are more multi-dimensionally aware than us. Without words.

Dimmed memory of Light is the cause of pain and suffering.
Fear in you calls out for what it believes it needs to feel safe.
A bottle, some food, a hug, a relationship, a bath, a friend.

Our mission is to help everyone, even a babe, go within to the Light.

The Radiant Inner Child and the Mystical

Children have mystical experiences all the time,
often without realizing this is occurring for them.

This happened to me as a child. I am not at all unique.

Children resonate to higher frequency and are not yet hard-wired.
Yet, without their full memory, experiencing a body is adventurous.

Imagine being you under these circumstances.
Oh yeah, you don't have to imagine! You know!

Those with highly sensitive nervous systems have quite a ride.

In Truth, we never really left anywhere. We just fell asleep.

As Enlightened Ones know, we exist as and in Radiant Light.

As we serve the kids, we feel into how cherished we all are.

The Call for Love by Children

Children are calling and screaming out to us.
Child bullying, suicide and homicide are astonishing.
Grown-up bullying, suicide and homicide are astonishing.
Children are asking us to believe in all of them and in all of us. Now.
We are unspeakably capable of meeting this call.
We must slow and listen within for peace and Light.
When we turn our back, we turn our back on us.
Help all ego/fear to relax. Help all feel safe.
Seek within for Eternal Light.
We cannot remember who we
are when we trust any dark idea.
Share a bright smile with a child.

Mission Awareness: "Me Specialness" versus Radiant Oneness

Be Lightly heart ~ full. Remember that everyone matters.
To save time, let's giggle and rhyme...
There is no worry for "the me" inside me,
...except when "I" forget(s) "the we" inside me...
Ego's "me" likes to shame or blame inside or out
and to make "me" great or even e"special"ly blue.
When you are feeling great or blue, remember Light.
We are deeply asleep when we decide we are
worth e"special"ly more or less than another.
As we give to "the we," we remember we are safe.
Love and kindness always comes from our being within.
Expect the wondrous! Feel Love's radiant vibes.
Ego is always unkind, angry or morose to self or to others.
Sample ego thoughts: "I want...or else!" And, "You are not great."
The gloopy or bossy glums are verification of the ego's veiled Love state.

God is Our Nature

Awakening ones know all that needs doing is
forgiving our own projection of separation!
Remember, we ARE God.
Ego says, "This seems wrong."
Ego is scared, sure its way is right all along.
Next time you are feeling not at all quite YOU (God),
ask deep inside, "What can I do to remember what's true?"

Awakening to Wonder from Inside

Since ancient times (no time at all really), our perception has been veiled to astonishing beauty. Our hearts, libraries, spiritualities and science labs are filled with evidence. Many humans, especially children, experience splendor that others do not perceive.

Life is a simple, practical, playful tool to support awakening to You.

To connect to wonder, open your heart and listen.
You will feel subtle oscillating particles within you.
Meditate upon Love's sounds and lights in you.

We have long quested to remember, to understand, our origin.
We are now remembering collectively that we are Love and Light.

From an early age, and due to an on-going mystical experience, I had an existential sense that this world where pain and suffering occurs could not possibly be my home. Because of this I would devote my life to inquiry and to trusting inner guidance. I would come to learn that legions before me have embarked on the inner journey, the same quest for Truth. Trust your heart connection to your core even if your mind objects.

Our belief in Light and Love's Divine Intelligence is not necessary. Truth is true. It simply is. Truth, Love and Light are blocked from awareness by our choice. Only a tiny spark of our awareness is here within an earthly realm of Light. There is a great deal confusion in the realm of our mind. Trust Love to guide.

A spark of our essence has journeyed into a made up world of "me" and "you." In Truth, no "us" and "them" exists. There is no harshly judging, external God. There is only Love and an incredible mix up in our mind about what we are and where we are. Never fear. Move quietly into your Still Radiant Core and ask why suffering exists. Attune.

Our state of being is no cause for the grumps.

We never really left the Truth of the Light.

Adventure into Light

Remember, only Love is real. Suffering and pain dissolves into supreme existence. Adventure into the heart in simple, yet astonishing ways. Trust your own Light.

Your mission, your purpose, is always revealed by your own heart and Light.

Just remember as often as you can: Sickness, death, hatred among peoples and a desire to destroy earth and its creatures and systems is not natural. Only a reluctance to trust Love causes manifestations of unholy horror.

A solution is eternal kindness, which helps everyone remember.

To awaken, judge no one. See only the Light.

Look beyond errors. All minds are veiled.

We are safely held in the Light of One.

When we leave

our bodies

we see.

Mission Understanding: Feelings are Extraordinarily Helpful

I spent last evening speaking with a young mother of two beautiful girls. Her dad died recently of illness related to chemical warfare. She is Light troubled to be torn up inside over a man's life being shortened by war.

Whether our upset is grief over war, illness or the passing of a loved one, food, education for children, care for the challenged, or the shifting of a relationship, our heart doesn't really want to be grief-stricken or angry so we may fight what we are experiencing, especially intense feelings.

All upsetting feelings are actually Love (Light) unrecognized. Allow these feelings. Honoring these feelings. Innocently.

Feel without judging what you or another is experiencing. Allow intense feelings to flow through you and dissolve. Be sure never to respond unkindly to self or another. You will hear this message often within The Mix Up.

We are learning that if, in our dire moments, we show our pain to the Light within the Light within shifts. We find that we are filled beyond any earthly cup's brim.

Our heart opens. (Our heart is our bridge to Divine Intelligence.)

Wait for your heart if you feel upset or unkindness bumbling in.

Honest awareness given to Light assists us all to waken.

Trust your subtle sense as a joyful spiral. It is a gift.

~ ~ ~

Awakening comes in Divine time.

Rest often. Love heart-fully often.

Affirm Children and Share About Ego

A child who is affirmed as good and beautiful, and who is made aware of the ego, the idea of "I am better or less," that lives in the mind here on earth, is a child who will become empowered to peace and not dishonoring the experience of all the others.

Help a child understand with language and symbols they comprehend. ...like sharing that ego is a beautiful little angel just a little unclear...

Exploring with children is a radiant adventure. Love concepts may need to be repeated often, in language, through play, symbol and story.

Light-full patience is a healing endeavor. (Patience heals us way more than them.)

As we adventure with all ages of us, ego's presence becomes obvious. Remember to always trust kindness. If you feel upset or guilt within, slow. Kindness remains the wise response. We each learn well what we teach.

Kindness may be a gentle, "Let's look in our heart." Or even a soft, "No." Or, "Let's make a different choice." Trust your heart. Forgive all upsets straight away. If there is an upset, allow the sensations to pass by holding a loving space through the discomfort. Now or later, have a gentle conversation. If you depart, leave with a Loving heart.

This, we soon realize, helps everyone.

Here's Why

How we respond to another teaches our mind how we believe we deserve to be treated. Unkindness blocks Light. Look upon all with heart. Upsets of any kind are a call for Love. Egos are filled with "special" stories of upset. This is not a worry. Let upset go, even if some stories feel like they are taking years to dissolve. We will allow strife in our mind until we recognize that we are fundamentally a radiant and Loving awareness. When we trust fear and guilt we give it our God-power. This is fact. If you find yourself appealing to guilt or fear within self, a child or an adult, remind yourself guilt and fear do not serve. Imagine a golden sun bow sphere surrounding us and wait for peace.

Unforgiveness

If you feel you cannot forgive, never fear the mix up.

One day, soon, you will and it will be easy.

Remember whom you really block.

Keep giving all upsets to the Light.

A Little More on Feelings

All beings born into this world have a split or veiled mind.
We do not recall what we are and how we got here.
This circumstance feels rather unsettling within us.

For the following, go inside and ask the Light to guide.

Bring to mind a tiny radiant irritation to your peace.
Imagine this upset as a cosmically reverberating clang.

An energetic clang is easily resolved if given its time.
Dance. Sing. Twirl. Go within to Love. In joy.
When we honor our experience, it dissolves.

We feel yet we don't yet remember our Truth. This is fine.
Emotions, feelings and sensations are helpful information.

Beneath an experience of feeling is a radiantly intelligent
Light that is entirely findable by those who seek for Love.

Go within and ask to be shown. The Light waits.

If our mind is caught in tales and upsets of the past,
tuning in is quite the adventure. This is why we rest.

Legions assist us from beyond the veils in our mind.
Angels weep at our radiance and efforts for peace.
Divine Radiant Peace is always present within. Always.

We are powerful co-creators of the Light.

Upsets fed with our Divine power feed our upset.
Upsets given to Love dissolve into Absolute Being.

Next time you're feeling an upset...
Rest. Breathe softly. Go inside YOU.

We All Know One

We are not body. We are not mind. We are Pure Awareness.
We are Light. Pain and suffering was never meant to be part of
Life. The cosmos, earth and children were given to help us remember.

Trust your joy. Trust your smile. We cannot mess up any endeavor no matter
how hard we try (and we try). It is purely fallacy that we need pain to know joy.
Ask inside. Do we need to feel murdered or murdering to know grace and peace?

The circumstance of peoples hating and destroying peoples, self and our
earth is not who we are. We are undergoing a profound and collective
awakening to this fact. In Truth, we never left paradise except within our own
mind. A multitude of exceptional teachings, including our most famous spiritual
documents, share brilliantly of the mind's ego/veiled state—its deep amnesia
of our fundamental nature as Light, as Unity, as Divine Radiance, and how to
awaken from this circumstance. Huge numbers are stepping forth to share
the wisdom of the Light. We hear about the Mayan calendar and a Biblical
apocalypse that speak of the awakening that is taking place within us.

The Greek meaning for "apocalypse" is "lifting of the veil" or "revelation."
The only revelation that exists is the revelation of Love's Divine presence.

In Jesus' native tongue, "sin" means "separate," a lack of love, a state that has
never been. In Truth, nothing is separate from anything else. We are aspects
of One Radiant Intelligence. The spark of us that is here has forgotten its True
Nature. (Ask deep within your being if you fully remember what you are.)
Because so many outstanding texts and teachers eloquently share about
our circumstance and how to awaken from our strange dream, The Mix Up is
meant as a supplement, not a substitute, for any tradition, teaching or teacher
that calls out to you in any given moment. Most of all, trust your own heart's
de-Light-full and wisdom, your peaceful intuition, your Inner Awareness.

Effective Prayer is Vibratory

Ask with all your heart to receive what is already given.[11]

When deeply heartfelt, this is perfect prayer.
Deeply felt thoughts create. Love's vibes are prayer.

You know innately how to go within and vibrate.

Love's Divine Intelligence guides us all perfectly.

~~~

Our "me" can be afraid of surrendering to Love's presence. Why?
Because Love is an inner experience we so often deny ourselves.
Love is beyond form and can be intense, so we are often afraid.

Trust what comes to your life as perfect for your awakening.

Comfort others. Trust your Love. Hold hearts of Light.

This is our mission for self, children and earth.

We're collectively surfin' the Love Wave.

Love knows naturally how to be free.

---

11   Quote from *A Song of Prayer*, a teaching scribed by Dr. Helen Schucman, scribe of *A Course in Miracles*. *The Song of Prayer* is available through the Foundation for Inner Peace (facim.org). It is included at the end of the 2007 Combined Volume (Third Edition) of *A Course in Miracles*, or can be obtained separately.

Trust Your Love

You are astonishing and Light.

You are cherished beyond measure.

We rest safely within the Heart of Divine Intelligence.
The Truth of our Divine Nature cannot be harmed.
We are radiant Light now and forever. This is fact.
Children need our help to remember the Light.
The fastest way to help us all is to **Trust Love***.*

Outrageous wonder patiently waits!

Peace Awaits

Trust that being respectful is always appropriate.

If your ego says, "Be rude," don't listen to it.

Forgive yourself if you treat another unkindly.

Remember, actual separation is an illusion.

We are kids in a toy store. They are Us.

What we vibe instantly affects. A fact.

Remember, we are of One Awareness.

Body is a temporal vehicle. One-as-many.

Ask for radiant forgiveness. This saves us.

See only a tiny lapse. A funky plunk.

While our ego may go wacky,

never hold too dear to fear.

There ain't no real huge dark.

Light is always bright right here.

Failure is Not an Option[12]

This world was over long ago.[13]

So, we don't need to worry.

We don't need to fear.

All we need is Love.

As we trust Love to

help us awaken,

we wake up

a lot faster.

We never left our Radiant Nature, so, rest assured,
we don't have much more unraveling of fear to do.

---

12 Title of a great book by Gene Kranz, well-known N.A.S.A. Flight Director (retired).
13 Science confirms what enlightened beings have been saying all along: Time doesn't exist, and space as we experience it is a holographic illusion. This is a dream. Suffering/illusion ended the moment it began.

Peace Is

No matter our worldview, most want inner and world peace.

Peace is nothing that needs to be created.[14]

Peace is what we are, by nature.

Yet, we do not re-cognize this by trusting ego.

We are, and we are immersed in, the Great Rays.

Factual references are in all our spiritualities, modeled by our most awake peace teachers and proved by science.

Most of all, peace is scribed in the fabric of our fiber.

World peace arrives when we trust inner peace.

This is radiantly universal. It's cosmic science.

We are coherently bright eternal Light.

~ ~ ~

Until we see the Golden Sun Bow Rays,

gaze deeply within a child's eyes to see

how we never really left Heaven's Light.

Never Fear the mix up.

Light is here. Right now.

---

14 A fundamental teaching. Peace is here now, within us. *A Course in Miracles* describes this brilliantly.

Honoring the Inward State

Be gentle with little ones and grown-ups who are venturing within.

*We may observe an adult or a child "zone out,"
and we may want them to "snap out of it."*

*Abruptly interrupting a dear Soul listening inside can be disruptive to
the nervous system, not to mention the individual may begin to become
self-conscious in an unloving way since not all remember we're all a-okay.*

*The "no-mind" state is deeply beneficial to our wellbeing.
Such a state is honored in many cultures and practices.*

*An individual in a peaceful inward state may be accessing
higher states of awareness that inform the quality of their lives.
If you feel he/she is in a downward spiral of darkness trust your heart to guide.
The Light can always be found inside, but if an individual mind is not yet
aware, it may be more helpful to guide her/him gently back to this world.*

*When it is necessary to bring an individual back into our world
before he/she might be ready to return to this realm,
ask inside yourself for what feels best to help them return
their awareness. Your intuition will always guide you well.*

Help all beings to know a peaceful inward state is Light!

*Assure the inner traveler that we are
beautiful, perfect and whole this night.*

Our Ego Tends to Respond First

Why is the world all a muddle?

*Unless we are deeply heart-focused,
our ego/fear-mind tends to respond first.[15]*

Ego is concerned that we are alone and unsafe.

Why?

*We do not fully remember that we are One
with full access to our Divine Intelligence.*

*Ego/upset is easy to witness in children.
Witness a little one becoming upset.
Ego is the part of themselves that
feels unsafe, afraid and alone.
A grown-up comforts fears
of its young, sensing the
child is feeling scared.*

*Children help us remember that every ONE of us matters.
A wise grown-up first honors an ego/upset of the child.
This is vital. Otherwise, ego may lash out further.
And still may! Ego upsets are easy to witness in
adults and in children. Observe us for awhile.*

*As a child comes to trust that a
grown-up is a safe place, (s)he
comes to deeply trust the
encouragement to
go within for
peace.*

---

15   Teaching in *A Course in Miracles*. There would be no need for enlightenment (i.e., ending suffering) if we remembered we are fundamentally One Radiant Intelligence fully awake and creating perfectly (i.e., without suffering or causing suffering for others/self) as Divine Intelligence/God.

Forgive All Error

We are utterly astonishing. Right Now.

Feel into our beauty today and every day.

Forgive our wearying, heart-blotching dreams.

Trust being vulnerable to what feels kind and helpful.

Always overlook error, your own or another's.

Forgive as we would forgive a small, terrified child.

Even if walking away, let go in Love's presence.

Trusting Love dissolves upsets from all minds.

This is called miracle working.

Heaven can now be felt.

And sometimes seen.

Fear is Afraid: Help It Smile

*We are aspects of One Radiant Intelligence. We created
competition and terrorism. Trust Love to end the dream.*

Our ego is afraid to look within. It is afraid it will find Light.[16]

*When we ask to be shown what is real, we will find the Light.
We realize our strange, terrifying dream of being "unOne."
At first, fear may seem to grow. Never fear. One is here.*

*We are utterly innocent of all errors because we
are dreaming. Many will be horrified by such a
statement because some lives seem to be filled
with the unconscionable by us or by others.
Yet, this is how we help ourselves awaken.*

*Always, it is vital to remind ourselves
that Light has never been harmed.*[17]
It is impossible to harm True Love.

*Love fear when you can. Fear is terrified. Help the fearful smile. And,
be aware. Fear may respond defensively if overtly loved or hugged.
Watch a child or a grown-up who is attached to a particular story.
They may not easily let go. Hold all in the Light no matter what.*

*Honor our beauty. Honor our grace.
Silent prayers may be most helpful.*

*Trust that a wholly Loving heart prayer,
your feelings of goodwill, are enough.*

---

16 *A Course in Miracles* describes ego's fear well. Ego refuses to see the Light, so don't take anything personally. Love/Divine Intelligence/That Which Supports Life recognizes what is real. That which isn't real (the absence of Light/Love/fear/ego) doesn't exist. Unkindness and disregard for Life is simply a fear that we are alone and unloved. Trust only our Loving vibrations and following our intuition to guide.
17 Look to any Enlightened Master for this teaching. Jesus appeared to suffer horrifically. He knew the world wasn't real and that his accusers didn't understand. He shared with us to look within in order to illuminate our mind.

Be Like a Child

I need Love before I get mad!
Quote by a highly aware and sensitive[18] five-year old.

Recently a radiant five year old was approaching a meltdown over the lack of oranges in the house. While it happens rarely, when this little one gets his heart set on something and it is not available, he can go into a downward spiral that causes angels to tremble. I happened to be in the dining area and began to dance and sing. I sang with jivin' movements about how interesting it is to wake up with no radiant oranges to be had.

Round and round and on and on I went. Two children were staring at me in disbelief. The upset child now had a twinkle of wonder and an almost smile. The room lightened. The particles of upset smoothed. Along came a group smile. I stopped abruptly. Two feet of glistening snow lay just outside. I pointed and said, "Oh my goodness! Have you ever seen what snowflakes look like? They are crystalline gems! Gorgeous! Bright Light!"

My tone, words and dancing signaled that it was okay for my friend to feel what he was feeling—sad and mad. The upset had been honored. When we acknowledge everyone, child and grown-up, as perfect no matter how we're feeling, our psyche, our ego, relaxes. Offer a radiant kindness in meeting upset. Validate the radiance of all.

Activate your own sense of beauty and wonder. Joy and wonder is always shared. Focus on something that helps everyone feel cherished, honored and enlivened.

We all need Love when we are sad and mad and glad.

Today, if you notice an upset, ask inside how you might extend Light.

---

18   A highly sensitive mind/nervous system is able to detect Divine Intelligence (coherent frequency) easily. However, without having our full memory of Divine Intelligence, the mind also feels the separation trauma deeply within – like a clang or an unpleasant pain or as radiating dissonance. Mind wants to attach story to *feelings* of upset, and the world seems filled with reasons/stories about upset. Trust Love to dissolve all upset.

Strengthening Trust in the Human Family

*When little ones and grown-ups are supported to communicate with
gentle language, and we invite each other to adventure within—
to Love—for help, self-trust and group trust expands. We find all
outbursts shortening dramatically and becoming less frequent.*

One day trusting our upsets ceases altogether.

*Adventure with vocabulary for kind communication.
As we practice, the benefits of Love become obvious.*

*Families are profound gifts for revealing where ego (fear) remains alive.
Fear-mind doesn't relax unless it feels safe. I've witnessed children calling
for a beloved parent, and then, when the parent is within touching range,
they lash out in words and/or with hitting, or they withdraw deeply within
not looking for the Light. This is purely an inner Light-blocking process
and is not to be taken personally. We are simply witnessing fear.*

*Our psyche believes the separation within our mind, certain we are alone,
unsafe and worth less or that others are worth less. A story of guilt, fear, shame
or blame may form or return. Forgive it. Ego presents to us as fear and all
unpeaceful states. Witness your experience in your family. Sometimes we want
a loved one close by, yet, we may also feel upset believing a perceived need
has not been met. Or, we want to be far away. Because all have a veiled
mind we might be feeding everyone's fear of being alone. Strive to help
each other to trust that we are all safe, perfect and beautiful right now.*

Everyone is doing their best depending on how safe we feel.

*It is helpful to never judge anyone's response in Life as
we expand our trust in our Light's Divine Intelligence.*

The Angels

Imagine a heavenly flock of Radiantly Glowing Angels.

This flock is alive with Life and Unconditional Love.

These Radiant Beings are always present.

They see only your eternal Light.

Ask to feel Angelic presence.

Angels are in your Being.

Ask to feel your Light.

Yay! Holy One!

It is done!

The Cape of Peace

Imagine the most wondrous cape possible.

Let it float into your awareness without thought.

Take a few moments to do this before reading on.

You will be using this cape to work miracles.

Feel its Light textures and materials.

Notice the shapes it contains.

What is the cape's color?

Is it a cape of many colors?

Feel the cape's essence.

It was made for you.

Wear this Light cape.

It is with you always.

You are Love's land's cape.

You are a Light's cape.

You are Always Safe

Never fear. You and I are always safe.
It is possible to mess up only in dreams.

Love is fail-safe. True power is felt in Love.
If we hate and fear and shame and blame,
we are mistaken. That is all. We need never fear.

Our True Love is always real. Our radiance is always real.
To awaken to the real, remove your mind from all delusion.
Trust Love's thoughts when your mind wants crazy thoughts.

Love's thoughts feel true.
Love's thoughts honor all.

Thoughts of rage and blame and shame do not
feel true in our heart. Let them go into the Light.

An ego's hate-state might feel pleasure from pain. Look again.
Hate is why we must go within. Inquire of you, "Is this Loving?"
If your heart says, "Nope." Trust that all is well in holding still.

The Light never doubts that it is safe. This may seem unwise.
So, bring to mind those who do not fear their earthly demise.

Whether you stand or run in time,
act in Love, for all is Divine.

Change Your System Default to Trusting Peace

*You know when you are feeling the Love. It's obvious. You feel Light.
In a veiled state, our system default is self-protective, self-defended.*

*We are having an experience of "separation."
In Truth, we never separated from anything.*

*As we recognize our Light, our heart begins to open. We realize everyone is in
the same we-craft at sea, riding the same we-wave. The Please Save Me wave!*

*Our ego is always making course adjustments, feeling into the safety-zone.
The difficulty is that the original premise is faulty. We are not truly separate.*

*What do we do when we feel off the Love course?
We trust Love's Light adjusting. We let bluster be okay.*

*The presence of some can feel disruptive to our
field. When I am in such circumstances,
I know that my own upset/fear/derivative guilt from
having my mind veiled is being felt.*

The whole world benefits from adventuring through the Inner Journey.

Visualize and feel us all in Radiant Light as often as you remember.

Trust that everyone wants to feel astonishing, safe and cherished.

The Ice in the Mind

Never under estimate the ice.
Wisdom by travelers to Antarctica

Never underestimate the ice in the mind.

The ice in the mind is our little self-will.

Shaming and blaming is icy fodder.

This cold, hard ice is not nice.

It masks Heaven.

Trust the Light.

Ice is fear, a sense to protect and defend the heart.

Melt the ice to find what's always been mightily right.

Give all stories of pain to Love's melting Light.

Love's presence fills all cups with beauty.

Heaven stands as the Real Warm You.

Manifesting

"I need do nothing."[19]

When we focus on gratitude and peace, we receive what is already ours. Love.
When we focus on shame and blame, we receive what has never been ours.

In any moment, either Heaven or the absence of Heaven is revealed.

Notably, trying to manifest "things" and "circumstances"
does not wake us up. There is nothing wrong with such activity
however it keeps us in the veiled/split-minded state.

Laws of attraction and repulsion function always. Our ego forgets what it wants.

As we focus on forgiving all errors what we need is provided.
As we focus on our heart's song what we need is provided
As we enter our heart's still core what we need is provided.

To manifest Heaven, we need do nothing. Heaven is already here. Now.
Separation and lack is not a natural state. Suffering is not a natural state.

Manifesting Heaven does not mean to shun activity.
Oh no, no, no...trust the Love vibe. We are free to be here.
Do what you love. Care for others on your way. The rest follows.

Be action with Love.
Be at rest with Love.

Light always guides without manipulation.
Trust that everything is perfect as it is now.
Gently care for the perfection that we are.

---

19 All Enlightened Masters share the knowledge that Heaven rests before and within us, we merely do not perceive it because our minds are so packed with ego/individualized thoughts. By honoring all Life and resting our minds, allowing Light to flood into our awareness, we quicken our collective awakening.

As we share what we are—Love's Presence—everyone is nourished.
As we share what we have, everyone is warm and fed.
As we share all the doing, everyone feels peace and joy.
As we share all the being, everyone remembers home.

The Golden Rule Gently Rocks Children and Grown-ups

Trusting the Light of all Life is essential to thrive.

Divine Intelligence literally cannot see error.

Divine Intelligence sees only Love's extension.

Golden Sun Bow Rays comprise and connect all life.

Extend Golden Sun Bow Love to fear and watch what happens.

Our heart sees that shame and blame does not work, so why do we engage?

Yet, even such states can be useful—for we will only tolerate so much existential pain. In pain we see and feel our inner blocks to Light. Suffering causes many to look within and to begin to trust Love. We all share the same stuff. Only Love and Light is real. In pain, we are calling for Love. When Light feels blocked, seek within, so that all may thrive.

Trust the Golden Rule of seeing only the Light in all Life.

As we adventure, the perfect situations come our way. [20]

---

20 *A Course in Miracles Manual for Teachers* says there are only three levels of learning. 1) Brief encounters, 2) Relationships that last for a period of time, 3) Relationships that last a lifetime, which are more rare. At each level, potential exists for a maximal amount of learning to occur/forgiveness/ release from guilt. All encounters of forgiveness/seeing only the Light in each other releases all minds from suffering.

Choosing Peace is an Inside Job

Because we are truly free, we

cannot choose peace for another.

We can only choose peace for ourselves.

Hold difficult (adventurous) relations in the Light.

Everyone is on their perfect journey for their awakening.

Trust peace within you, and allow others their own experience.

Our only need is to transcend the fear and guilt in our own mind.

We model right energy when we are non-reactive and gently

collaborative and supportive. Others naturally learn from us,

as we from them, because we are fundamentally One.

Labels of Love?

We are in a (mind) world that
loves to break down, to classify.

Ponder gently labels of any kind.
Feel into the energy of given labels.

Without making judgment, become lovingly
aware of our labeling tendency. Just observe.

Ask within, "How does this label feel inside?"
Ask within, "Does this label's vibe honor Light?"

All labels and our attachment, our belief in labels,
blocks our Light's radiating glee. This is a felt sense.

Sometimes it doesn't feel so easy to let go of labels.

All we need is to ask Love's presence to show us what is real
and to look for the Light as often as needed—for we are deeply
asleep and rather deeply attached to some ancient feeling labels.

All labels began after our amnesia of One.

Absolute forgiveness is needed. An overlooking.

If we hold to a speck of an unLight labeling of mind,
guess what? We keep our awareness of Light veiled.

Ask, "Is this label a Remembering Love label?"

If it is not, forgive it with all your heart's might.

Free Will and Kids Helping Grown-ups

The one thing the Enlightened Ones cannot do for
us is to eliminate our fear of waking up to our Light.

We must ask within for Love, for
our own True Nature, to help us.

Be us child or grown-up, our ego/fear-mind is very alive.
As we help each other feel valuable and necessary our
psyche relaxes its hold on fear, guilt, shame and blame.

Children are deeply trusting of Love, Light and grown-ups.
And, kids usually give up stories of pain faster than grown-ups.
Children are also adept at accessing high states of awareness.

Our True Nature is helping us as gently as possible, through kids.

Adventuring with Our Veiled Mind

Peace and joy is our natural state as Pure Awareness.
Another part of us, an unreal, but very real-feeling part,
is deeply afraid that we are alone, broken and unworthy.

Or, that someone else (or a group) we don't happen to like is.

When we believe that we, or others, are not whole and worthy
we tend toward making choices that reflect false awareness.

In Truth, our awareness is deeply veiled to astonishing wonder.

Human perception (our ego/fear-mind) is detecting little of
the splendor that we are and that we are immersed within.

Ask a scientist or your heart.

Due to our deep focus on Love through the eons, our DNA,[21]
our Divine Blueprint signal-receiving device, is waking up.
We are deeply tuned into higher states of awareness.

Our perception is expanding.

Evidence for the highly sensitive (expanding) nervous system is everywhere.

Children are more awake upon arrival.

We're grasping that grown-ups are
the ones who are more veiled.

Slow down. Honor you. Listen with heart.
Gently listen to youthful expanded beings.
They are communicating significance with us.

Are we listening closely? We are being sung Home.

---

21 Research wonderful scientific exploration confirming the switching on in the last few thousand years of long-switched off DNA. The University of Chicago has done research on at least two genes, ASPM and Microcephalin, related to brain growth/expanding awareness.

The Lazarus Effect[22]

*Remember the biblical story of Lazarus being raised from the
dead? Lazarus' family is a teaching tool for us. The family's
grief at the passing of Lazarus was overwhelming.
Jesus recognized the opportunity for a closer examination of the illusion of death.*

While Lazarus returned for a time, his body would eventually pass.

True healing is about recognizing Love and eternal Life.

Healing is about acknowledging the Light of all Life.

Physical healing of a body is always temporary.

The physical realm is always temporary.

Healing is about remembering Love.

If you are ill, Love everyone mightily.

If another is ill, Love everyone mightily.

Ask how you can take gentle care of you.

Ask how you can take gentle care of another.

Your heart will always guide for how to do this.

Sometimes we are to care for another.

Sometimes we are to care for self.

Always we are to love patience.

---

22   This title is from a beautiful film called "The Lazarus Effect." The film explores the HIV/AIDS epidemic in Africa, and how many are being helped by the newest medications.

Divine Intelligence Communicates

*Divine Intelligence knows I love animals. It uses all
my languages to get through to me.
Here is an example. A few nights ago I had a dream.
I was in a lovely little shop. The shop was a browsing adventure.
I came upon a gigantic stuffed alligator and grinned that child grin,
ear to ear. A sparkling Light stare. I was now a little one
encountering an extraordinary creature never before seen,
striving to integrate this wonder in my world.*

*A woman came from behind and asked me the
alligator's name. I had no idea!
The thought of name had not crossed my mind. I touched
the alligator's soft side and moved toward its full head. The
woman reached down to a tag on the alligator's ear.*

The ear tag said "Lily." This got my attention! I woke up.

*Lily is a name I use frequently. Indeed, the first name I was drawn
to work under to assist folks to focus on the Inner Light is Lily Wisher InnerViews.
I interview people with gentle, focused questions around an area
of interest to them. The process triggers the memory of stories of Love,
goodness, beauty and Inner Light awareness. From a healing and life
expanding perspective, this endeavor has been wildly
successful because awareness comes from within
participants themselves and beautiful stories are shared.*

*In addition to the dream, right now in my life, two children
dear to me have been mentioning alligators and crocodiles.
They want me to draw them! The reputation
of alligators and crocodiles caused me pause.
I felt the need to do some research!*

Alligators and crocodiles are powerfully assertive medicine.

What might Divine Intelligence be sharing with me?

I tend to be one who gravitates to a quiet inner place.
Being in the public eye is a "place" my ego avoids.
Perhaps I need to be more assertive in some way.

Bring to mind signs and symbols in your own
life and the languages you gravitate toward.

What might Divine Intelligence be sharing with you?

Dissolve Energy Blockages

Have you ever felt a subtle or strong energetic release in your body?
(I'm not actually speaking of what might be the most popular one.)
It is an interesting sensation. There is no doubt when it is occurring.

Perhaps you have had a massage or an energy healing session and felt an
energetic release, a muscle relax or a deep breath release spontaneously.

Energetic blockages occur in our mind before they lodge in our body.

A Course in Miracles explains that all upset is identical energetically,
from the slightest feeling irritation to the most intense experience.
Believing upset disrupts our awareness of Love's eternal presence.
Strongly held-to beliefs that block Light may manifest body dis-ease.

As we shift perception to Love by asking for help from within during an upset,
the sensation of upset dissolves because it is…yep…never real to begin with.

All upset revolves around not feeling safe and cherished.
When we feel unsafe Light is blocked from awareness.
The nervous system activates. We call out for Love.
(Bring into awareness the fight or flight response.)

This is the moment to remind our self of Light.
Remind yourself you are wondrous and wise.
Remind yourself all egos are just a bit wacky.

To help release blocked energy, it is helpful to focus on heart or belly
breathing and to tap on acupressure points, including Emotional
Freedom Technique, and many other stress relieving tools. Find
what works for you to regain a sense of calm presence. [23]

---

23 For maintaining basic balance, drink plenty of water, eat whole foods and exercise/move/dance/
flow and giggle as often as possible. When our body is in balance, it is easier to access higher states
of being.

If you choose to tap on acupressure points, here are affirmation ideas:

Please flood my awareness with Light. I rest safely in Heaven.
Please help me remember the Truth of our Radiance.
I am safe and held in Light and Love. Always.

The Recession

One day not too long ago I received an email from a friend who knows what I do for a living—encouraging people to trust their Inner Light. She is also a peace teacher. Something was up! She was emailing from her cell phone while on a Sunday adventure with her partner. They were meandering and had stopped at a local organic bakery for some refreshment. My friend shared that the owners of the bakery were not particularly friendly or concerned about serving her dietary needs. (She has food sensitivities.) She said the proprietors were deeply concerned about the recession, believing in lack.

Believing in worry and feeding its vibe, rather than offering it to the Light, amplifies vibrations that attract more experiences that express the fear that we are not safe. Worry says we, or others, are profoundly guilty. Focusing on lack brings lack. We train our mind to trust illusion. Voila, the Law of Attraction is always at work. Yet, never fear! We are never upset for the reason we think.[24] We are existentially upset because we forgot what and where we really are! We forgot how amazing we all are! Worry does not wake us up. Lightly release all worry to Love. Forgive all worriers. (Ultimately, all forgiveness is self-forgiveness.) When we release our silly vibrating delusions, asking Light's Divine Intelligence to flood into our awareness, we quicken enlightenment.

Assure worried minds that everyone is always doing their best.

Ask what we can do to help reveal everyone's Inner Vibrating Giggle.

~ ~ ~

Whatever is up is perfect for our awakening. All circumstances are gifts, opportunities to help. Honor feelings of upset to help them dissolve. It is wise to forget about the story. Notice your feelings. Ask within if a feeling feels like you, like your Radiant Self...or not.

If it doesn't, ask within for the feeling to shift, so we can feel everyone's Light.

---

24 This teaching bears frequent repeating to our heart. It is well discussed in *A Course in Miracles*.

See everything, every single moment of Life, as an adventure into Life. As we trust the adventure, we open an existential space for new information to flood our awareness. We naturally become less demanding and more collaborative. We find our natural compass bearing is peace and joy and wonder. Time[25] frees our mind of illusion. Feel into the concerns of others. Ways to connect that didn't seem obvious will appear.

---

25   *A Course in Miracles* explains the use of time brilliantly. Time is for overlooking error and seeing only Light.

Our Amnesia

Do you wonder why the world is all a muddle,
...even when you are doing your best...?

There is a reason.

We forgot something important.

You are radiant.

I am radiant.

All are radiant.

And, we are One.

To help us all, trust Love.

We are astonishing and deeply cherished.
We are not broken, nor have we ever been.
As we Love the world, we remember the Truth.

Everything is One.

Share your resistance with the Light.
Let your discomfort be okay.
Do not resist upset.
Allow it to flow
through by
paying it
no mind
at all.

Believe in Us

Love is written within and around.

These are not words for ego. Oh surely nope!

Ego gets all fuggle buggle when we speak of Truth.
It begins ramble scrambling about your truth, my truth,
personal truth, science truth, Absolute Truth and on and on.

One is proved by Love's inherent Light.

Can you feel this?

If you live to your core One Whole Love,

YOU are awake and not in fear.

You are ready to see the Great Rays full time.

If you are uncertain, there is adventuring still to be done!

Union's perfection is unremembered, but not for long.

Share all concerns with Source. Ask for radiant help.

A dreamtime is ending. We are waking to wonder!

~ ~ ~

Kindness to all causes all kinds of inner quickening.

Squeeze My Hand

Squeeze my hand. Come on. Stay with me.
Dr. Laura Bowman in film Beyond Rangoon. This sentiment
is echoed in the hearts of children all around the world.

In the film Beyond Rangoon, broken open hearted over the loss of her husband and young son in a brutal murder, physician Laura Bowman travels on a wave of grief to Burma (Myanmar) in 1988, during the 8888 Uprising.[26] Burma is embroiled in terror, our radiance unremembered. Laura wants her pain to heal. She wants to find purpose again. She does. In the terror and chaos, she knows to keep looking within.

Laura trusts the radiant value of life and responds with grace.

Laura is a doctor, a healing practitioner whose hands hold life. [27]

The tissue that forms our human hands comes from the heart's tissue.

Wow.

Like a surgeon or an ice climber gently cares for her handy instruments, knowing her passion for life is genuinely expressed through her hands, care for your hands today. Express your gratitude for your instruments.

Take good care of you and your hands.

We are held in Love.

Feel this in your hands.

---

26   Source: Wikipedia
27   For a healing hands story, check out the wondrous autobiography *Gifted Hands*, the story of Dr. Ben Carson, a gifted neurosurgeon.

Light and Comfortable or Decidedly Uncomfortable

Have you noticed how in some circumstances you feel comfortable?
Have you notice how in some circumstances you feel uncomfortable?

Awareness is important. Trust this inner felt sense,
but don't judge it or those who seem to prompt it.

Divine Intelligence is always a felt sense of peace.

Situations where we feel less comfortable are where
the most Radiant Light/Divine Intelligence is needed.

Please do not judge or feel guilty for anything within an uncomfortable situation.

Offer upsets to Love's Presence that is always within us. Now. Forever.
Gently allow uncomfortable thoughts and sensations to pass through.

Focus on your breathing, which may take you beyond breath into stillness.
Removing our attention from upset is extremely effective for healing.

Trusting the Light is powerful for, yep, enlightening.

Here is an adventure! Or, if you like, create your own.

In a triggered moment, bring your awareness to your breath.
It is impossible to be reactive when we're focused on our breath.
This transports us to a Divine Intelligence-minded state of awareness.
Visualize a golden or a sun bow-colored Sphere of Light in your heart.
See it expand outward at a comfortable rate. Feel its light and warmth.
This golden or sun bow-colored Sphere encompasses all, including you.
Continue to focus on your breathing as you get used to this practice.
As we practice, it grows easy to respond to worldly circumstances
and hold a beautiful space where our own Divine Intelligence
can be easily accessed. Be inspired by what gifts transpire.

Courage and Love's Sun

Last weekend I witnessed a seven-year old trust her Divine Intelligence.

Mila is a dancer who has been preparing for months for a season of performances. On a day before she was to perform she came down with a bad flu. Her school called her mother, who contacted me to retrieve her from the nurse more quickly than she could reach her. When I arrived Mila was deeply upset. She ran to me in tears, grasping for Love and comfort. Yet, she was not looking for comfort from me because she didn't feel well, though this was clear on her pale, drawn face. Rather, she wanted to be healthy for a family dinner at her favorite restaurant to celebrate her hard work.

I did my best to offer words of comfort. "You never know!" I said. "You may feel well by this evening! We truly never know! Love is always holding us!" This seemed to calm her heart a great bit. The evening did not find her feeling better. This sweet, radiant, uncomfortable child snuggled on the couch with her mom, her attentive brother and me close by, all of us watching Tooth Fairy, a joyful film about Love's Divine Intelligence.

We never made it to dinner. The next day, Mila was pale, still not her full radiant self, yet she wanted to dance. We told her in no uncertain terms she did not need to perform. However, she was resolute. On this morning, a gentle grace and determination enveloped this small child that felt far beyond her young years. Her mom and I exchanged wincing glances, trusting her, and went about preparing supplies.

This angel, Mila, danced her heart out. Twice.

Melting into her mom after each performance.

We had just watched Love in action.

Love's Sun

Love's Sun is everything that exists.

There is nothing that is not a Sun of Light.

Guess what this makes you?

For a glide of glee, adventure with the teachings of Jesus, Buddha and every single Enlightened Master. Most of all, check within thee.

If you've ears to hear, this is sounded in every year by those born to remember: Love is the real you.

We cannot remember we are the Holy Sun of One if we choose to not see the Sun in Every One.

Strengthen Inner "Glowareness" through Art and Play

*When presenting for healing circles or workshops, I arrive with a bale of toys.
I call these quantum toys because they hold potential to trigger glowareness.*

We explore with magnets, jelly and spheres and animals and the cosmos...

*For exploring glowareness, it is vital to be aware that
all sensations come from mind, not body. This is fact.
Therefore, there is vital information in all sensation.*

The more we practice inner glowareness, the more we become gloware.

*Pain, including physical distress, always comes from within the mind.
Peace always comes from beyond mind. It comes from glowareness.*

*As we move within, to the core of our pain,
we realize only Light and Love (Glow) is real.*

*Children and grown-ups may enjoy drawing, painting, or using art or dance
in some way to strengthen our glowareness of the astonishing wonder
we are and rest within. Grab paint, markers, crayons and paper!
Have no plan. Simply allow your glowareness to direct the show.*

*If you feel stuck within or cannot seem to tune into clarity,
breathe, move, stretch, oscillate, twirl and listen within.
Whatever you feel, move it with feeling. It will lighten.
If you feel joy, move within the joy. It will uplift you.*

*You can move all by yourself, and many wondrous
movement teachers exist. There is a practice called
Sweat Your Prayers. Or, check out gabrielleroth.com.*

You are Divine Radiance! You are oscillating Light!

Simon's Divine Intelligence

I have a beautiful dog, named Simon.
You'll read of him here more than twice.

Simon guides and guards me well.
He stands at the back door a lot.

He is looking for intruders like
Darling Deer and Sweet Skunk.

When he spots our brothers and sisters, he barks.
He is calling to me to let him out. And even more,
he is calling to the darling sweet to be aware of him.

An ego mind says, "If Simon was smart, he wouldn't bark or howl.
If Simon was smart, he would silently walk to me, nuzzle my hand
and gently coax me to the door to let him out to chase the deer,
of which I would be unaware because he's given me no sign."
(Simon knows I am more likely to let him out if he is silent.
He is never let or left outside when he makes a royal fuss.)

The heart says, "Simon's Divine job is to care for his family. He protects me in the
way Divine Intelligence has asked him to. He helps me know what surrounds."

His job is not to maim or kill in fun. In his heart, he knows we are One.

Dog lives to inform, to protect the body-tribe and to remind us to play.

We won't need dog bodies forever.
Yet, in the world of time, they are great.

We are Doggedly Divine! We are Waggin' Radiance!

Trust that all are worth loving in a way Holy way.

Creative Politics

Bring your radiance, your Light, to all moments.

Help our local and our global politicians.

These beings take the cold and the heat for us.

One day my sister-in-law and I were driving to the train. For some reason I had politicians on the mind. I feel compassion for politicians, so I said, "I wonder what would happen if, before making any decision over conflict, everyone involved in decision making, and in criticizing those decisions, on both sides, gathered together in a single location, sat together and smashed their faces into coconut cream pies."

There is wisdom in participating in joyful sensory experiences together, especially when we need to make decisions or are feeling an upset.

When we take ourselves too seriously we become very muddled.

The world would shift in an instant if for an instant, at the exact same moment, everyone simply focused on Divine Radiance.

Many efforts are occurring globally that are doing this right now.

When you wake up every morning focus for five minutes on Light.

Adventure daily with Divine Intelligence stimulating practices.

Feel peace within. It is always present.

Swathe the earth in golden radiance.

Knights of Light Heal an Ancient Wound

In our defenselessness, our safety lies.
A Course in Miracles

We are all Knights of Light
dissolving an ancient wound.

We are all peaceful warriors.

Our ego fears defenselessness.

Ego always fears its demise.
Ego always fears True Love.

It forgets Heaven.

Divine Intelligence knows death is impossible.

Love trusts Love.

You are a Knight of Royal Radiance in need of no defense.

You are an eternal Light. Heaven is only masked.
As we become like little children gazing at self
and at the world with wonder, we awaken.

Here are two films portraying worldly
knights adventuring to awakening:

Kingdom of Heaven
2005 Ridley Scott
Orlando Bloom

King Arthur
2004 Antoine Fuqua
Clive Owen

Going Within A Mighty Heart
(Recommend reviewing the next two pages before practicing.)

Our heart is an activator of Divine Intelligence.
We vibrate with Divinely Intelligent information.

For a gloriously effective approach to activating your heart,
it is recommended to begin this exercise with closed eyes.
Ultimately, we can do activities of this nature almost
anywhere, with heart open, eyes open or closed.

Such a practice can be used simply to relax, or to enter a peaceful,
open state of higher awareness. It can also be used to help re-center and
re-balance in order to move effectively through a challenging circumstance.

Put on favorite loose, cozy clothes.
Be in a comfortable, peaceful space.
Perhaps light a candle or two, or place a
few objects nearby that warm your heart.
Have a glass of water or herb tea nearby.
Hydration is very helpful to hold resonance.

Focus gently on your breath.
Ask peace to support you.
Gentle the busy mind.
Tell ego it is safely held.

Gently sit or lie down into calm, peaceful awareness.
Pillows can support back/neck/knees. Be comfortable.

Allow your body to relax as you explore dissolving tension.
Begin by breathing gently and communicating gently…
"Feet, you can relax. You're safe here." And exhale.
"Legs, you can relax, you're safe here." And exhale.
"Belly, you can relax, you're safe here." And exhale.
Move up, through and beyond the top of your head

To your toes, let go in peace. Gently exhale resistance.

Going Within A Mighty Heart
(continued)

When you are fully relaxed and feel ready
(If you're not already fast asleep, which is fine!),
bring your awareness to your Mighty Heart.
Feel its pulse. Feel its pump. Feel its vibration.

Ask Love to activate your heart in a helpful way.
Express that you want to tune into Divine Intelligence,
that you are wanting to know, to remember the Real You.
Have no expectation or assumption around this request.
Simply trust that Divine Intelligence always responds.

Remain here for however long it feels natural to do so.
When you come out of this state, be gentle with yourself.

Drink plenty of water throughout the day.
Staying hydrated helps us hold resonance.

Love yourself for being willing to explore in this way.
If you are contemplating a circumstance in your life,
adventure Lightfully for insight with The Mighty Heart.

As we travel along the path to enlightening,
we may find life's circumstances calming.
We may find things jiggle up a bit.
All is always for our awakening.
As we trust peace and love
every journey is peaceful.

We can return to our mighty heart
in any eternal moment we choose.

Thankfully, time is occurring at once.

Releasing Shame and Blame

Truth is blocked when we trust shame or blame.
Our thought-feelings are immensely powerful.
They are quantum resonator creators.

Forgive and Love them gently.

Release them into presence.

Only wondrous gain is found
when we go within to Light.

Only Love is real.

Love is within.

Hug all egos.

We need lots of hugs!

Love away fear and struggle.

Egos dissolve quickly in the giggle.

Can you feel it?

I can too.

Adventuring as Love

Trust Yourself as Love.

We are each and all whole and perfect.

Now.

Forever.

There is no exception to this.

Only unremembrance.

You cannot make a mistake.

If you feel you have, forgive yourself straight away!

You are Divine Radiance.

Truth is written in our hearts. Truth is written in the wavy~particles that comprise the essence of our being. Your heart's wisdom guides you perfectly. Wisdom is always an inner gnosis, a felt sense, deep awareness. Ours may appear to be separate journeys, yet they are not. As we trust our Love, and as we uplift and encourage others, releasing expectations and assumptions for what "should be," the veils in our One Mind dissolve.

Love is the realm of miracles.

We remember we are not separate and it's fun!

What could be better than playing together!

Mirroring

As Divine Intelligence, our internal state becomes manifest outside.

What we focus on within becomes manifest in our world.

...the entire cosmos and beyond...remember what we are...

God's Great Rays...WHOLE LIGHT...Source...I AM THAT I AM

...universal mind brings forth adventure and coalesces matter...

Yet, do not worry at all about what is in our world (if you are).

Love sees only Love, even if our veiled mind doesn't agree.

Simply pay attention to that which fills your mind's might.

Send Light when you find yourself focusing on blight.

Become aware of the judgments you hold.

When we judge, we attract what we judge.

See only our innocence. This is what's true.

~ ~ ~

When something presents in your Life that doesn't feel right, ask
inside what you are judging to bring forth this circumstance.
Be honest and forthright, just now, to release unkindness.

We may keep thoughts private from people,
yet, be sure to know that our judgments are
never private from ONE Divine Intelligence.

We draw in what we judge to heal misperception. We ask for it.

This is why the Golden Rule is given: SEE ONLY LIGHT.

Adventuring Beyond Upset

I had the awareness early in life to regard all circumstances, especially painful ones, as gifts. I would come to call these gifts adventures. While my soul did not accept pain and suffering as normal, I knew I was not "at victim" to them. I was on an adventure. Such awareness allows discomfort to pass through unjudged.

Because some adventures feel far from gift-like when we are in the midst, it helps to keep the frequency high. Using a description like "adventure" is far more uplifting to our Light Spirit than a description like "problem" or "difficulty."

Embrace all life's experiences and all inner sensations. Ego's fear simply cannot process joy and peace. When we remain in peaceful joy, we are safe, no matter what our external appearances.

Bring to mind stories of when you focused on Love during an upset. Draw on memories to strengthen you in uncomfortable moments.

A sample: I had the flu recently. It was one of those astonishingly adventurous bugs where couldn't stand up straight, and, if I did, I threw up. (Sorry for the graphics.) I found myself lying prone on the bathroom floor making up comedy routines about how "paradisiacal" this experience was. Not! What came to heart were those going through illness, chemotherapy and other circumstances and how folks face great internal distress on a regular basis. I recalled a dear family member who died in extreme discomfort at the age of 34, months after the birth of her second child. My baby brother died of painful blood poisoning when he was three months old. Hearts break wide open during such times, yet there is also often a feeling of being safely held, fearless of death.

Resources sharing how Love works:

The Tiger in the Snow and Life is Beautiful Films by Italian filmmaker Roberto Benigni demonstrating the power of trusting Love.

Mr. Magorium's Wonder Emporium Dustin Hoffman plays a playful Jesus/Buddha like character. Mr. Magorium knows to keep his focus always on the Light.

When You Find Yourself Upset

You are never upset for the reason you think.[28]
A Course in Miracles

All upset, no matter the scale, is a call for Love.

When you are upset, if you are willing, ask a question:

*Am I able to be present and to be helpful to self and to others
if I believe in myself and everyone around me as good and kind,
or if I am contracted and defended, judging the world and myself?*

All unkindness and lack of Love is a call for Love.

Give your mind time to return to a peaceful state.

*Will your mighty heart to recall: There truly is no real past!
Help ego relax and remember that we are utterly safe.*

*If the mind objects to peace, forgive it.
All concern is fear for our wellbeing.
Remind yourself that we are all perfect.
Come together in peace, always in peace.*

*We are radiance.
We are bright.*

We are One Whole Light.

---

28 *A Course in Miracles* and many other teachings implore us to recognize that all upset is a call for Love. Explore inwardly for how to meet the call for Love (our own or another's) in a helpful way. Whatever we feel moved to do, we do it with Love for our radiance rather than with anger against (fill in the blank). Trust that everyone is calling for Love. It is worthwhile to remember and share often with others that while attack doesn't harm our Divine and Unified Radiance, it does delay our awakening to the awareness of it.

Adventuring Beyond Fear/Ego

A fearful mind blocks the Great Light.
Don't worry. We all have fear-mind.
Fear is nothing at all to fear.
Embrace your fear.
Love it away.

Ego is the fear of Love and Light and nothing else.
Ego is the fear that we are alone and separate.
Ego manifests circumstances that attempt
to convince us that we are not safe.

Nothing is further from the real truth.
We rest safely within coherent light.
Our full radiance is within.
Look always within us.

Ask to Know the Light.

Ego wants us to look outside for solutions.

As we trust peace within ourselves, we naturally
respond with peace and grace in the world.
Look to any number of role models for
evidence of the Truth of this fact.

You are courage.
You are strength.
You are radiance.

YOU are found in gentle, loving kindness.

Compassion for All Rocks and Lightly Rolls

You are doing a great job! Can you feel this?

You haven't had your full Divine Memory
for what may feel like a seriously long time.

This is huge. What a ride.

We're always doing our best with what we remember.
Acknowledge how kind you have always been.
Acknowledge your pain and confusion at times.
(And don't believe the pain or confusion for a nano-second.)

Legions of Angels are hugging us right now. Here. Always.
Often those in the more dire appearing circumstances,
from our perspective, are the most trusting of Love.
This is because they are sensing what matters.

You matter. I matter. Compassion matters.

Love yourself the way Divine Intelligence loves you.

Divinely. Wholly. Perfectly. Now. Always.

Forgive. Believe in your Light.

When you feel a great boo, hold another in radiance. Journey in. Bring
to awareness how we love the following list of dreamtime players when
they serve our needs. And, when something doesn't seem to be going our
way, these beings take our ego's heat. Financiers – Attorneys – Doctors –
Leaders – Politicians – Teachers – Builders – Media – Parents – Celebrities.
The list goes on. If you are triggered by any, share all kooky vibrations
of upset with Light. Ask Love to help us heal and know what is real.

Compassion gently rocks and lightly rolls.

"Take" and "Slack"

In climbing the words take and slack help save lives. Here's why. When a lead climber is ascending a rock face, she is relatively unprotected should she fall. To secure her form to the route along the way, she sets protection in rock crevices or around rock outcroppings or vegetation. The rope is threaded through gear in a manner that allows it to move freely. If the lead climber takes a fall, she has a chance of being halted by a combination of well-placed gear and a quick response by her belay/climbing partner.

Belay means roughly "to secure."

A climbing partner, called a belay or a second, stands at the base of the route (or along stops). He or she is feeding out just enough rope for the lead climber to climb relatively safely. If the second extends too much rope and the leader falls, (s)he will fall significantly farther down the rock face because rope is slacking below. This can be deadly. Because of this, a leader and a second are in constant communication.

Climbing partners are connected by a rope, which offers a felt sense of what is happening, and, ideally, by line of site (vision) and also by voice (sound).

Imagine such a scene in your being. In addition to the felt sense of rope and line of site, climbers use specific voice commands. (Sometimes line of site is not available. And, if it is a windy day or a route curves, voice communication may also not be available. For our purposes, we'll assume voice communication.) If the leader believes there is too much rope slacking below, he will yell out, "Take!" This word signals the second to bring in the rope, yet to be sure to not pull the leader off the route by taking in too much. If a leader needs more rope to climb, or if he is threading rope through gear and needs a bit extra for this purpose, he will yell "Slack!" Great sensitivity, listening and intuition are required for safe climbing. Climbing partners are usually friends who resonate well.

If you feel an upset, trust your inner belay. Secure your heart in Light.

How do you communicate to build trust in your relations?
How do you ensure that your sensitivity is enlivened?

How might you take up or offer some "slack" to yourself or another, extending a deeply needed Love line to all Life?

You are a miracle easing out lots of miracles.

How Can I

How can I? … is a beautiful question.

This morning, as I was writing at the computer, a little one asked me,

"Where's my mom?"

My ego's instant response was muddled at being interrupted during an intense moment of writing. It sought to express a quick, "In her bedroom."

But Love's radiance stopped me warmly.

Love helped me realize this was a beautiful learning opportunity.

Together, right now, we would shift our reality.

Kids always want to know where their parents or closest caretakers are. They are little air traffic controllers always looking for a safe landing. Grown-ups are their comfort. They also love to ask adults for help, trusting with their Heart's Light that we will kindly and gently assist.

It is our job to work with them around the question, "How can I?"
"How can I look first within to be sure I am acting with gentle respect?"
"How can I look inside my heart and adventure with (fill in the blank)?"
"How can I remember what my mom or friend or teacher taught me?"
"If I need a huge hug and some gentle encouragement, how can I ask?"

To help us in the world and also to remember that we never really left Heaven, we can look deeply inside ourselves, as well as around us, for safety and help.

As we inquire within, "How can I?," and, as we trust only the inner responses that honor everyone and also help ourselves to feel kind and at peace, we are saving ourselves hundreds, perhaps thousands, of years of painful learning. We are dissolving the veils in our own ONE mind.

Heaven awaits!

To Enlighten Quickly

The question "How Can I?" (on the previous page) is significant.

The psychology of always trusting kindness is deeply transformative.
Trusting kindness and peace literally wakes us up from our amnesia.

Consider this, how we treat another is exactly how we treat ourselves,
for we are fundamentally One now believing we are many "bodies."

(Remember, we are not really bodies, we are One Pure
Awareness temporarily animating bodies. This is fact.)

If we are rude and dismissive, we teach ourselves
that we deserve be treated rudely and dismissively.
Such choices keep Heaven veiled from awareness.

Our veiled mind attempts always to defend.
If you find yourself in critical, unkind mind,
forgive yourself and remember that
you are perfect and whole and
that so is everyone else.

Today, pause and breathe as often as you remember.
Trust that Heaven's Light is within you, always present.

In a triggered moment, ask yourself how you can
show up as love, as joy, as peace and kindness.

Remain silent until you are sure of your Light.

A response will always flow naturally.

(Remember, a kind, "No, thank you,"
can be as loving as, "Yes, please.")

Jelly Belly

When you feel like jelly, trust the sensation in your belly.

Trust your intuition. Trust your inner felt sense as guide.

You cannot make a mistake when you trust Light.

~ ~ ~

Divine Intelligence is always communicating with us.

Are we paying attention to Life's radiant messages?

There is much written and shared about this subject.

If you are not already familiar with it, perhaps explore the Chakra System.

Chakra means wheel or vortex of frequency. Chakras are everywhere.

Our bodies are formed from at least seven main vortices.

These vortices are sometimes thought to be in our body.
They actually dimensionally came before/transcend it.

Our physical form and our subtle bodies are holograms of energy,
densified frequency. Our bodies are made of the light from stars.
(Ancient Egyptians believed our souls are stars. How cool is that?)

As we attain higher awareness we transcend density
and ascend into finer, refined or rarified awareness.

Ultimate awakening transcends all form manifest states of being.
This might sound (and feel) a little freaky from our perspective
because here we're so used to traveling in heavy bodies. Yet,
when we leave form, we recognize the limits of physical form.

Adventuring with Heartful Language

We are hard on self and each other beyond any reason.
It is easy to see the fear, shame and blame of others.
What we hide well is our own shame and blame.
We must bring our inner suffering to the Light.

If you share your thoughts with people be lovingly aware. Ask within your heart if this would be helpful. Find those who will mirror your radiance and not support your fear story, yet who will also not criticize you or your story. Ask them if they would consider holding a safe, loving space. (By all means, forgive all lack of safety. We're all learning together.) Our ego-mind needs a hug, not confirmation of its false belief that it is not safe and not deeply cherished. Ego/fear can be tricky because it is so bodily attached. We may think we're being supportive or supported, yet we end up feeling worse, stuck or sticky inside. Pay attention to how you are feeling. Peace and joy is our natural state. Yet, no one is ever wrong. Everyone is doing their best to be helpful, so don't make others wrong, or beat up on yourself for asking for help and then find you are not getting the support you feel you need. Everything is an adventure, including rejection. All is used by Love. And, truly, we are the ones who asked to have an experience of being an individual with our own thoughts and desires. This is why we don't always agree or fully remember Love. Sometimes sharing our hearts with trusted friends helps us remember the Truth of our Divine Radiance, yet sometimes sharing keeps fear intact.

Be slow and communicate in a heartfelt way.

As much as you can, remember to not take story too seriously.
Obviously some stories may feel quite challenging to release.
Ask the Light to guide us. Ask what a Loving Being would do.

Adventuring with Common Sense

Here's a question for your heart's mind.

*Do you feel wise, happy and clear when you are
sad or mad, or when you are glad and at peace?*

*Sad and mad is nothing to be concerned about.
Offer your mind comfort. Share that you are safe.*

*Imagine golden sun bow radiance.
Light is always present in and around.
Go within your heart's radiant awareness.*

*Our heart is far wiser than sad or mad-mind,
so our heart never makes sad or mad wrong.*

Ask questions that are on your heart.

*Or, simply and gently ask for peace
to be restored to your awareness.*

Wait for the inner shift to be felt.

*Now or eventually, depending on how attached
mind is to a particular story, you will feel clearer.
You will know naturally how to respond to
any circumstance that feels adventurous.*

*We can never know how another will respond.
This is truly and actually none of our business.
The wisdom is simply to trust our own Light and
the Light of all with whom we travel on earth,
regardless of how we feel about a personality,
preference or trait of our own or someone else,
at home, at work, at play, in all our communities.*

Good Works, the Inner Journey and Awakening

Children and earth are great reminders of why it
matters to do good works in this world.
When we don't take care of children, earth, self and each other we feel this neglect
inside. Why? We are a shared, a joined, awareness. We are a consciousness of unity.

Engage in the world with your heart's peace, joy and delight.

We come to recognize the purpose for good works.[29] They help
us dissolve sensations of guilt and fear and shame within our own
awareness. We come to realize that we <u>are</u> our brothers and sisters.
As One, we relate deeply and may come to be in the
same circumstance as those we may temporarily seem to be assisting now.

Enlightened beings such as Jesus share often that...

Good works have nothing to do with actual guilt and shame! We are and
have always been innocent except within our own deeply judging mind.
In trusting kindness, we release our mind from its prison-like belief system.

The adventure is that we are always One. Our heart feels this. Ego is deeply
afraid that we are alone/unloved (whether or not this is admitted). When we
do not honor THE ALL, we feel an existential sense of dissonance/discomfort.

As we enlighten, we are naturally shown our blocks to (fear of) the Light.

Every day, as often as you can,
gently set aside your own cares.
Set aside the cares of the world.

Go quietly within.
Ask to remember.

---

29   Jesus is clear that good works not done with peace, joy and a full heart are better not done. Actions not undertaken with Love and joy actually block Light from our awareness. For example, imagine an adult or child being forced to do something he/she truly cannot stand in a particular moment. Mind and heart resist the Light that is present. It is vital to honor the intuition of an individual and assist each of us to honor the flow of Light within. We are each guided from within toward good works that resonate for us. As a mind enlightens, we find joy and peace in virtually any Light affirming activity or circumstance.

Oil Pastels, Auras and Divine Soul Mixing

*If you love radiantly colorful artistic adventures,
head for the local art store for some oil pastels.*

I call these grown-ups crayons.

Locate some quality paper for your glowing imaginings.

During quiet time, take out your paper and your pastels.

Cover the paper with all sizes of marvelously colored hearts.

Be flowingly creatively drawing your fully hearted page.

Now, set aside your grown-ups crayons.

Imagine yourself as lots and lots of these hearts.

Imagine others as hearts not designated as you.

*With your sacred fingertips, rub the colors of the hearts
so they blend together. For example, a blue heart and a
yellow heart rubbed together will create a green glow.*

*The glow is like an aura. We radiate and are immersed in auras.
Auras[30] are frequency fields that surround and permeate form.*

We are always blending with each other in the Oneness Field.

*Play with seeing auras as you move through your days.
Gaze at an object and allow your vision to soften.*

*Contemplate your aura's colors mixing with the
aura of another and the whole of all radiant Life.*

---

30 Explore Kirlian photography, a photographic process that records the aura. Many humans, including children, see aura fields. Anyone can see auras when we relax deeply enough into pure awareness.

A Snowy Forest Walk

Divine Intelligence is within and around us always.
D.I. knows how to be and what to do very well.

Recently I was walking in a snowy forest with a sweet young boy.
Above us a clump of dead leaves was falling through some branches.
I pointed out what was happening. My friend felt sad. I said, "Oh sweetie!
This is perfect! Leaves know just when to fall to the ground to be recycled."

This little one's heart began to sparkle with curiosity and wonder.
We can only imagine the impressions flooding an opened heart!

Like the falling leaves…

The Light always knows how best to create new life.
It is the same with our lives. Light knows what works.

Falling leaves are not endings. Our moments of free falling.
Our Divine Intelligence is present to Light our path into Love.

How could you uplift another who feels like Love's Light is scary?

Divine Intelligence sees the value in all Life, rising or falling. Honor Life.

~ ~ ~

Like the perfection of the falling leaves…

Many years ago a teacher said to me, "Water is pure life. It doesn't care how
it is used, only that is it used." Ask to be used by the Light. Trust what comes.

When we trust the Light, we work smarter and play joyfully and with relish.
When we honor a natural unfolding of Divine Intelligence everyOne thrives.

Help another to trust that Divine Intelligence
is taking care of us in the perfect way for us.

(Be heart-full that your ego doesn't interject its own agenda.)

Adventuring with What Works for *You*

I spend a lot of time with radiantly hearted kids.
They love when I stroll and mosey around the house
singing about how wonderful they are and how grateful I
am for their friendship as we move about our play and tasks.

Children feel my heart and love creative play. A grown-up might think my singing and twirling is cute for a little while and then find it intensely irritating. (My voice alone may be irritating!) How do you help people around you feel valuable and cherished? How can you help people around you to feel valuable and cherished? What can you do to help yourself feel valuable and cherished? We are having individual-feeling journeys—journeys where our telepathic abilities are rather dimmed—so it helps to communicate in other gentle ways. Find out what helps those around you feel seen and Loved. Imagine families, communities and the whole world in golden radiant Light.

Bring to mind a memory of when you helped
someone to feel jolly great about themselves.

Give everyone, including you, the space to be our radiant self.

Adventurers and Teachers

I have spent glorious years of my life surrounded by individuals who spend a lot of time in the wilderness in unforgiving environments, such as climbing high mountains and traveling at the poles. Hardened (softies really) climbers and adventurers are aware of what surrounds and their inner state of being. They understand the value of self-care and respond calmly in circumstances that would have most of us peeing in our pantaloons. Many ingeniously employ very little to accomplish a whole lot. These are beings I want around in an emergency to keep all calm, helpful and laughing. (They are some of the funniest and smartest people I know.) They tend to spend a lot of time by themselves or, if not alone, in silence. They recognize that no "body" is special in nature's Divinely Intelligent world. Nature is deeply unbiased. This is wise to ponder.

Spending time with wise extreme adventurers is a great canvas for exploring ego. (Ego is the aspect within that feels separate, self-protective, self-defended, and more or less special than others. Ego wants desperately to stay alive.)

If you want to wake up faster, it is great to get out into nature to feel your ego (blocks to your Light) up front and personal. Nature plays no favorites. No single body is more special. Ego is quickly revealed in the remote. And, our Lightness can easily be seen. We notice swiftly when we feel safe and help others feel safe and valuable. And, we notice swiftly when we are uncomfortable to downright terrified for our being.

The slightest inner discomfort to the most intense terror is a call from within. When we honor our discomfort it is easier to be aware and to ask for help.

With calm observation, it is easy to locate wise teachers and adventurers on this exquisite planet. Those with a sixth, seventh and eighth sense are radiantly honoring their inner awareness. Such beings listen deeply within and to the input of others, including those who are new to environments. Divine Intelligence knows that those who are new to a place may see things in a Light way. Something radiantly helpful may be shared.

If you are interested in outdoor or extreme travel, many wise guides exist.

Gifts of Divine Intelligence

You tune into Divine Intelligence all the time.

You are good at many, many, many things.

Radiant areas where you naturally shine.

Are you especially kind or focused?

Are you a curious learner?

A great game player?

A wondrous chef?

A teacher students adore?

Do you love kids or animals?

Do you enjoy fixing stuff?

Taking stuff apart?

Do you work Lightly with hair (I deeply admire this skill!)?

Do you love math or dance or music?

Do you help people feel valuable?

Freely share your Divine gifts and smiles.

Support a child to thrive doing what they love.
Locate the best possible teachers and support.

Encourage immersion with heart (not with busy, critical ego mind).
Our heart is our link with Divine Intelligence. A natural flow ensues.

Basking in Cosmic Wonder

This world, our dreamtime, is an astonishing, if strange, miracle,
a miraculous hologram made possible by Divine Intelligence.

We are resting safely within Love's effervescence!

Try this cosmic adventure…

Head outside on a clear or relatively clear night. Draw a deep breath and exhale deeply. Gaze into the cosmos. When you feel peaceful, lie down gently on the sphere of the earth. (Make sure you will be lusciously comfortable for lying in the ground.) Feel into the soft or the solid-feeling earth beneath you. Gentle your attention to tune into the cosmos, the higher harmonics of color, sound and vibration around and within you. Offer your glorious radiance an invitation to be lightly and deeply felt. Feel the Great Sun Bow Rays we rest within at all times. For a few moments, close your eyes. Focus on activating your heart's crystalline magnet. Such focus helps facilitate higher awareness. Activate a vibration of gratitude within your heart. When you are ready, gently open your eyes. Focus your eyes on empty space. Softly gaze into the infinite expanse.

Gentle your heart to trust deeply within your core that you are safely held.

Allow your intuition, your felt sense, to guide.

Feel your being naturally aligning with the pulse of earth and the cosmos.

Have a lovely, grace filled evening!

Perhaps share this adventure with a child or a friend or partner.
Position yourselves slightly apart to have your own experience.
Or, join hands and lie down together and gratefully feel alive.

If you find yourself focusing on an object, a star, a planet, or
a thought or feeling, this is perfect! Notice what is coming up.
There may be a wondrous insight here, a message.
Perhaps you are simply feeling peaceful. Love what is coming into your awareness.

When you are ready, return your focus to peace, and, again, drift into the Light.

Adventuring as *Feeling*

Holy radiant feelings! Trust your intuition!

Trust your feelings, your felt sense.

Our felt sense is helpful information.

We are immersed in Pure Awareness.

When we feel an "odd" feeling, the wisdom is this:

Be mindful to not attach story to a feeling.
Simply be aware of what you are feeling.

This is your Light sharing awareness information!

Your heart will guide for how to process awareness.

If needed, be heart-fully kind to ego (all upset), yours or another's.

Hug ego. Call it Hugo-the-ego in trust.
Assure ego that it is safe and perfect.
(Sometimes silent assurance is best.)

Honor all individual feelings and experiences.
Honor your own feelings and experiences.
Discounting our Love or our fear is unwise.
Share all awareness gently with the Light.
In time "all odds" will dissolve in peace.

When you are in Hugo, i.e., not at peace and in joy and wish to return,
gently rest your thoughts. Offer adventurous feelings to the Light.
Upset will always pass because peace and joy is our nature.

We are radiance always and forever and ever.
Yet, when we don't honor our experiences,
even our adventurous ones, we teach
we are not radiantly worthy of Life.

Adventuring with a Sword Carrying Knight of Light

(Playing with a Star Wars-loving four-year old taught me this one!)

Bring into your awareness a stunningly gifted sword fighter.
This bright Knight of Light loves battling (pretend) monsters.

Can you find this scene in your awareness?

Now, envision the following:

A sworded event outside.

With Light Sabers, of course!

A bright and sunny day.

This Knight of Light believes his pretend monsters are real. They look real!
He is attempting to maneuver the monsters so they are facing into the sun.
(If they are facing into the sun they will be blinded, not easily seeing the Knight.)

Can you find this scene? Can you feel it in your Light wavy particles?

A sword fighter wants his back to the sun to be able see the monsters.
This dreaming Knight of Light knows that if he is facing into the sun,
he cannot clearly see his monsters in order to slay them.

For awakening, what is the wiser position?

When we face into the Light we cannot see monsters!
They were never there to begin except within dreams.

Go within to...the Light...

Wowsa!

What? Not a Body?

We are not body.
We are not mind.

We are Pure Awareness.

We are Radiant Light, not body.

Trust loving kindness. Listen well inside.

Peace always emanates from within. Yet, peace
does not interfere with our free will to disregard it.

Next time you are with a group or a person you don't particularly like,
focus deeply within your heart holding a vibration of Light and gratitude.

Share the following silently, inside yourself:

You and I are not separate. We are radiant.
We may not resonate as personalities,
yet we are whole and perfect right now.
See all thoughts in your mind within a sun bow.
Check the integrity of your thoughts. Trust feeling.
Speak only if your words are in integrity with radiance.
Otherwise, simply hold your focus on peace and service.

Pay attention to where your awareness takes you when
you call upon Love's Absolute Certainty of the Light.

Actively applying such a practice to any circumstance that
feels adventurous in any way will lead to outstanding insight.

Adventuring with Children

Ever wonder Why Children?

*…especially when they take a whole lotta years to grow up,
and never leave your heart, and, in some cases, your home?*

They are gifts from our <u>A</u>bsolutely <u>D</u>ivine <u>R</u>adiance.

Children remind us of our forgotten innocence.

Our ADR knew they would come in handy!

They would remind us of the Truth of what we are.

Our mind gets a little confused as we "grow."

Still, always, we are all Divine Radiance.

Spend time with kids. Young and old.

*Enter a child's world. Unconditionally.
(Except to keep bodies safe of course!)*

Be the child's joy. Be the child's pain.

A child's pain is never hidden.

A child's joy is never hidden.

As we relish adventuring

we forget about pain.

A Temporary Vehicle

Physical form is a temporary vehicle for Divine Intelligence to explore. We don't even need to look to awakened beings to have this fact confirmed. Check out the myriad of accounts of out-of-body experiences and near-death experiences. Death isn't real.

Better yet, go inside. You will be shown when your awareness is clear.

It is astonishing how often we trust guilt and fear over Love.

Trusting Love's vibrations quickens our awakening

Our world, our hearts, are calling for Love.

Children are calling for Love.

Living in Love is simple.

Two resources I love calling for:

Ultimate Journey by Robert Monroe
A super fun and easy read. Monroe founded the world famous Monroe Institute. Robert's work is exquisite regarding our limited perception and that death is not real, i.e., only the physical form passes away. The Light of our Soul continues its journey.

Stalking the Wild Pendulum: On the Mechanics of Consciousness by Itzak Bentov
Mr. Bentov writes brilliantly on how mind/consciousness functions in our universe.

Adventuring with the Incomprehensible

Wherever we look toward spirit or science,
we are told that space-time is an illusion,
a real feeling and appearing place,
that is actually nowhere to be.

...hmmmm...

Can you feel it?

Perplexity?

I can too.

A spark of our Spirit is within a dream, a holographic projection.

Shown by science, shared by the enlightened.

A celestial wonder of incredible degree.

Two years ago I had a vision. The vision came like a wonder.

As the thought to separate, to individualize, was born,
a celestial container was made to hold the dreamer.
A radiant holy grail of Light came into form.
An exquisite sheath of wavy dark pink Light,
a highly penetrable veil of astonishing wonder.

All we need to do is to have the thought To Know
and our awareness begins to transcend the sheath.

Adventuring with Sun Bow Bright

As Dr. Seuss might say,

Feel your Light. It is sun bow bright.
It will always guide with angel sight.

The world of "you" and "I" is calling
to remember the wonder that we are.

Interestingly, no one else can chose wonder for us.

This would have been done, but the gift was truly given.

We are truly free.

Free to dream any dream.

Heavenly or hellish.

Because our power is vibration, our intention for holy might,

when we believe deeply in fear, we experience fear.

Yet, only Love is real. Only a veil remains.

...hmmmmm....

Trust the Light Within All Life.

Remember the children.

We are all radiant kids.

Trust the Inner Light.

Adventuring Beyond Guilt

*A most basic understanding for awakening is the
importance of releasing our mind from guilt.
Dissonance within a mind that feels guilt is overwhelming.
All errors/shame/blame come from confusion in our own mind.*

*Guilt blocks the Light, peace and joy that is always present.
It is adventurous to awaken when steeped in guilt and fear.*

This is why we are encouraged to Love. (Way less guilt and fear.)

Ego always gravitates toward guilt, our own or another's.

This is why the teaching of forgiveness is given.

It releases depression, rage, anger, frustration.

*As we overlook error, our own or another's, the guilt
in the mind soothes and smoothes into nothingness.*

Where does this guilt come from?

*We have a strongly held, now mostly unconscious, belief that we walked out of
paradise and will be punished in returning. Bring to mind the biblical story of
the prodigal child and the Loving Source of Life. The "me" is the only judge.*

*Trust stillness. It is profoundly helpful to accept that in our veiled state
feeling guilt and having guilty-thoughts is a fact of our make-up.
Forgive and trust Love. Honor integrity because it helps us.
Let go of guilt by honoring all beings, including you.
We are seeking for our memory to be restored.*

When we dishonor, we affect our own self.

Beyond the Inner Victim

*When we feel at-victim to (fill in the blank) we are giving our radiance
away to something that has never existed, i.e., to something else!*

Remember, we are Love. Love is everything. Love is all.

There is no something else. There is only unity.

Our Divine Radiance never changes.

*While it is fine to have our stories,
trusting in stories is a delaying stop.
Dreams always fade, sooner or later.*

*We can look to stories in our own mind and
that fill the world that are blocking Light.*

Love all beings. Love the stories.

Trust in only what is Light.

~ ~ ~

Be certain.

Here.

Now.

To Love the World

Forgive the world.

Know the Light.

Radars of Divine Intelligence Give Generously

A few nights ago my sister-in-law and I retrieved her five-year old from school. He said, "We have to go to the store to get Buzz Lightyear™!" Buzz is a wondrous character from the Toy Story films. The child was adamant. Sue and I looked at each other and headed for Walgreen's. We had no idea if this child would find the treasure he was seeking. In fact, in our search, we discovered the toy section was being re-made. Most shelves were bare. The scene looked grim. Then, we turned around. This child's radar fully attuned. He found Buzz buried behind another action figure. His excitement was infectious. And, the action figure in front of Buzz was perfect for his best friend, his sister.

Sue uses her intuition for when to say yes to the kids. She knew on this day that giving this little one what he was asking for was important. She said later she would have driven to other stores in the galaxy seeking for the superhero if he hadn't shown up where he had. (Buzz is used as a symbol of remembering Love in Sue's household.) Grace ruled. Buzz was right where he was expected to be. This is how Divine Intelligence works. It knows exactly what we need and when we need it, without fail.

A Course in Miracles says, "You must give all to have all." Our radar must be attuned in absolute faith. Parents tune in this way.[31] They remember to feel that we matter. This opens the space for miracles. When we hold back in a moment of intuition, we sleep.

The giving of money is a small thing. We should do this easily.

It is the giving of self, an undefended gentleness that heals.

In trusting Love, we remember Heaven's embrace.

---

31 When we *feel* that something is important, Divine Intelligence naturally honors it.

Experience

Honor it.

Celebrate it.

If necessary, forgive it.

Allow the world to be.

Allow the self to be.

*The self will always seek the
Inner Light when it is ready.*

We need force nothing.

Surrender to the Light Inside.

~ ~ ~

*If you love the wisdom of the enlightened,
experience the intention beyond the words.*

Love everything as it is.

Such an idea seems horrific to us, yet it frees.

*Notice how you feel inside when you are in discontent.
Belief in discontent perpetuates an illusion of discontent.*

Give your discontent to the Inner Light. Ask to remember.

Celebrate your experience and let it go into the Inner Light.

Our Eternal Nature

Bodies pass away.

We don't. Ever.

Our Divine Radiance, our God-ness, never changes.

*We have never been in trouble or
unsafe, except in our own mind.*

Now, we don't have to pretend to die to remember.

Adventuring with the Undiminishable

*Not one wave-particle of our Truth is diminished
by any dream of fear, guilt, shame and blame.
The adventure is that, until we trust in our innocence,
we remain deeply veiled to the Truth of our radiance.*

Go within.

Ask to know.

Trust your Light Self to guide.

You will not fail to remember.

And you will compress time.

Adventuring Beyond Time

*Every Spark of Light, every Soul, born in this
world has their Divine Memory partly veiled.*

We do not fully remember our Light origin.

*Even Spiritual Masters must restore their memory.
This is what Jesus was doing all those years.
This is what Buddha was doing all those years.
This is what we all are doing all these years.
Unveiling our mind, going within to the Light.*

Each moment we trust Love, we are within the Heaven we never left.

The time is truly and only now.

Not "now" in that we need to panic if we forget!

"Now" in that we can only remember Truth in the moment.

*As Jesus in A Course in Miracles, and all spiritual teachings and science, so
eloquently points out, "now" is the only time there is because, in Truth,
in Light, time doesn't exist. "Now" is the closest it is possible for
us in our veiled state to feel eternity, to access eternity,[32]
the state of Pure Awareness, our natural state.*

Time seems linear to us, but it is not.

*When our mind is drifting into past and future,
we are literally nowhere but in our own dream.*

---

32 Space (as we know it) and time are dreamtime constructs. There is no such thing as past or future.
They are illusions of the veiled mind, a tool for Love's dreamers to dream. Our awareness knows that
in the "now" moment we are safe. We are escorted gently from this world when we depart our form.

Adventure with Thriving

We thrive when we all feel dearly loved.

We don't thrive when we don't feel nearly loved.

It is the same for everything.

We deserve to thrive.

Go within.

Thrive.

Cherishing the World

Cherishing is easy when we are hanging with those we love and who love us. The adventure comes when we are not feeling the Love vibe. What are we to do? We are to Love. We are to change the way we feel about the world's response.

Indeed, for the brave to ponder, when we draw what doesn't "feel nice," it is a gift to remember to forgive and to go within to the Light.

As we hear the call for Love, the world shifts naturally.

Love is fail-safe. We simply cannot "go beyond" the veil if not in Light.

Love is the strongest resonance because it is the only real resonance in existence. This world where "us" and "them" and fear and pain seem real is not real at all. We are free to create any dream we want, even dreams of fear. It's a choice.

*An upset is a very powerful alchemical moment.
We are literally feeling the original separation within.*

Ask to feel Love and to open your heart to the world.

As we look deeply within to the Light, sharing our upset with Love, it will pass through. Depending on how attached our mind is to a particular story, a situation may re-appear until we choose to release our own fear, shame and guilt around it. No one can do this for us because we have chosen to be here now.

*We see others to the degree we grasp our own Light. Forgive.
(Forgiving doesn't mean we become a punching bag.
We can walk away. Simply walk away in Love for all.)*

*We are Divine Radiance, unspeakably cherished.
We are indescribably free to dream of not Love.
Yet, nothing can harm the Truth of our True Light.*

Recalling Love and Light is the foundation for religion, science, healing, stress relief, personal growth, yoga, spirituality, nature exploration, breath, meditation, prayer...

We save the world every time we smile with heart.

What About Personalities and Old Wounds?

*Let go of worry about personalities and old wounds.
We have never been hurt. Yep. Seems incredible right?*

*If we desire to dissolve upset and connect with our Inner Light, the wisdom is to Love
and to enter stillness in all cases. Allow old wounds to dissolve. The radiance that
we are, regardless of whether or not our ego/split/veiled mind believes it, is real.*

If you are feeling an upset, simply go within and allow the shift into Light.

*Our heart and Legions of Angels and Beings beyond the veils in our mind implore us
to trust Love. Difficult circumstances are profoundly helpful. We are always seeking
to activate our awareness of the Truth that we are Absolutely Divine Radiance.*

Thank your difficulties for showing you who you really are.

All beings and all experiences are teachers.

Don't believe unkind stories. Offer them to Love.

It is helpful to remember...

*We manifest exactly what we need to wake up.
In our dream of separation, we will not ever feel
fully at Home, unless we go within to the Light.
When we do this regularly, it grows easy
to Love everything and everyOne.*

Remembering Our Perfection

We have all been part of upset. Once we honor our feelings—
ideally without projecting onto others, but if we are not perfect in
this we forgive everyone, including ourselves, the circumstance shifts
naturally. We often forget what upset us in the first place.

Bring to your awareness the memory of such a story.

I had such a circumstance occur several months ago. I was
attempting a kindness to an animal and a profound misunderstanding
occurred. Another's guilt was triggered. Unkind things were said
to me. During the interaction, I felt prompted to leave.
After I departed, I went within myself to calm and to share my upset with Love.

We can never control how another will respond. In triggered situations,
it is wise to bring into our awareness to not take anything personally.

(Check out the book The Four Agreements by Miguel Ruiz.)

I knew with certainty the beauty of both of us and to forgive the awkwardness in
the situation. I trusted it would work itself out sooner or later. Forgiveness works fast.

Self-forgiveness is actually all we're really doing here in this world.
We are releasing our mind from guilt and fear over a separation
from each other and from Love that never actually took place.

Human Projectors

In our veiled state, we humans are inner projectors and outer projectors.

Play with the Inner Projector...

I'll use me as an example. I'm more of an inner projector.
When I feel a fright inside, I tend to be hard on myself.
I may eat too much chocolate or food in general,
fueling the inner sense of not being a-okay as me.

Play with an Outer Projector...

When we feel like we're not getting our "rightful" way,
we can go into a terrible tirade about this and that.
We talk about what just doesn't seem nearly so fair.
We radiate poopy glare. We glare in utter despair,
which feeds our inner sense of not being a-okay.

As we become aware of our not very nice glare,
~ ~ ~ be it radiating inward or out ~ ~ ~
all that is needed is to ask Love to come forth.
It is already here! It just needs our permission.

When we remember we never left Heaven,
there is nothing to do except to trust intuition.

(Remember, upsets are always coming
from an inner sense of not feeling okay.)

Light Up the World with Your Worth

When we extend Love to another, we remember our own worth.

This is great community service!

Loving all wakes us all up.

Vital Awareness...

*If the mind is deeply entrained toward not believing its own
worth or another's, it may physiologically feel good in the
short term to be unkind/harsh with itself or others.
Check within to ensure that your responses are kind and honoring toward all Life.*

*If someone feels calmed or peaceful (high) by engaging in violent acts toward self
(substance abuse, self-violence) or by projecting on others with critical and violent
thoughts, words and/or deeds, consider seeking assistance to help the ego calm.*

*Receiving assistance does not mean we are broken. We have never
been broken. This is what enlightened beings are sharing. Our acting-
in or acting-out moments are simply moments of feeling shame,
fear, guilt or blame, whether or not our mind accepts this.*

*When we surround ourselves by those who affirm our Light to us, without calling us
broken or wrong, fear relaxes. Healing comes from within. Good friends can help.*

*We are whole and perfect, beautiful and innocent.
Only our mind is veiled to our astonishing wonder.*

Finding Divine Intelligence

Our ego says thinkin' rules.

Ooooooooops!

Listening within you rocks!

You are Divine Intelligence.

You always know what is helpful.

If you have a question, explore this:

Activate your heart's crystalline magnet.

Enter a space within you of deep gratitude.

Willfully place your question into your heart.

Know with certainty an answer is already there.

Gently listen and contemplate without thoughts.

An idea (or ideas) will enter your awareness now or later.

A response from Divine Intelligence carries a sensation of peace, a vibe of "Yep, this is cool. This feels Life honoring."

Trust that, when done with heart, making a mistake is impossible.

See One, Do One, Teach One

Gently bring into awareness your definition of learning success.

If you are extremely adventurous, write down what comes into awareness without thinking about your definition. Just trust what comes to heart.

Now let this definition go. You can retrieve it later if you desire.
Turn now to contemplating the following teaching technique.

In experiential education, we use an approach called

See One, Do One, Teach One

First, students are shown an activity/a new skill. A demonstration is made.

Then, students actively participate in practicing the activity/skill until they are sufficiently practiced to teach it to another learner.

Finally, the first students teach the activity to new students in order to strengthen their own remembrance and muscle memory of the skill. This style of learning is naturally service-oriented. Everyone benefits.

Try the following as it relates to deepening your Inner Journey.

See One
First, bring to your awareness a kindness extended in an awkward circumstance. Recall past stories of your own and those you love, or role models you admire throughout history, that reflect peace, kindness and heart-felt awareness.

Do One that Naturally Teaches One
An opportunity will soon come your way when your ego could choose to be less than kind to yourself or to another. In this circumstance, be only kind to all. This teaches your mind that you deserve to be well treated and cherished.

Bring awareness back to your definition of learning success. If we choose the goal of awakening to our Light, we can use any now-precious moment of peace to go within.

One Radiant Team: Trust You and Everyone in All Situations

It is vital to feel confident in our gifts and in our value within a group.

Establishing group trust and maintaining a strong team-oriented, supportive environment allows everyone to flourish and expand their unique capabilities.

We never know when our gift or another's might save a life.
Trust and awareness helps us all to stay alive and to thrive.

Outdoor educators use the following technique to help students learn from mistakes while supporting them to maintain and strengthen their self-trust.

Instructors open with a sincere, heartfelt compliment for the student.
Together, student and instructor gently explore the learning opportunity.
Instructors close the learning opportunity with sincere, heartfelt thanks.

Adventure with this Light-full technique on you
when you're not fully feeling your radiant Light.

Start with a compliment for you.

Assume the best. We all are great.
Remind yourself that you are perfect.
Allow peace to penetrate your awareness.
You may feel an inner release or recognition.

Explore the learning opportunity.

If you sense you could have handled something more heart-fully, listen within for guidance. Our Light always knows what is helpful and easily forgives the past. Release the past. Focus entirely in this moment. Trust what comes from within. You will know perfectly how to proceed.

End with a compliment.

Thank yourself for being willing to look within.
Thank the Light for its presence within all of us.

Is Independence Possible?

We are not separate from anything at all. Nor have we ever been. A fact.
Golden Sun Bow Rays are what we are. Our True Nature is always present.

Our ego believes independence is a real thing.

The only real thing is Divine Wholeness.

Independence from Divine Intelligence is impossible.

Yet, we are free to dream of freedom from Divine Intelligence.

The adventure in our "freedom dream" is that we are in rather a collective muddle.
We love feeling independent, yet we have scared our self and each other to death,
all because we have temporarily covered over our enlightened Divine memory.

Explore what independence means for you.
Now, remember to trust Love's presence within.
Remember to trust that only interdependence is real.

Bring to your awareness what is required to keep your body alive. A whole lot is.
Independence is a story that keeps us chasing our tail looking for Heaven.

Follow your heart's song. Real Life lives fully free in peace and joy.
Embrace life in a physical body. Breathe, twirl, weep, laugh, sing.

We are Divine Radiance.
We are free to dream in pain.
We are also free to wake up and
create in resonance with Light.

We are deeply afraid of Freedom's Light. We are afraid to let go within,
believing only a shadowy prison lies there, when only Light is real.

Hug Hugo-the-ego! This is how asleep we are. Rather deeply.

Golden Targets

Simon is my Golden Heart Retriever.

He teaches me everyday how to be wise.

This year, I was teaching a four-year old, who is now five, to throw a ball.

To...you guess who...

Yep.

Simon-the-Great-Tennis-Ball-Catcher!
(Did you think I was going to say "Retriever?")

My sparkling friend Jackson focused deeply.

We clasped Mr. Ball to our hearts and tapped.

We imagined connecting our hearts to Simon's.

We gazed in gratitude style on our Golden Target,

where Mr. Ball was to go—into Simon's choppers.

Explore where your chaotic tosses
can become pure Light trajectories.

Adventuring with Horses

Horses are gentle, wise animals of prey. Their flesh serves as food for others. Because their survival depends on awareness, horses are extremely sensitive to their environment. They feel into what is going on around and within. Always.

Equine nervous systems are highly sensitive like many human beings born these days.

It is a wise soul who learns the language of the horse.

Horses are clear, honest, open communicators. Knowing to collaborate with all life, they will mirror their environment.

Spend time with a radiant horse. He/she will reflect to you what you are really feeling, not just what you think you are feeling. Without judgment. He/she just knows.

Spending time around horses, in safe and honoring ways, assists our own nervous system calm and entrain to the Light.

The life span for a domesticated horse is approximately half the life span for a horse in its natural, environment, running wild and free without border and with its family. (Horses are herd animals born to roam together.) This isn't shared to bring forth guilt for having domesticated horses. This is shared to emphasize that as we each trust our nature and heart's song and honor these in others, we trigger our joy-mind, our peace, our eternal radiance. As we do, we set up everyone for success. We find that as we are more honoring of people and the world around us they reflect back the same to us.

Many humans with behavioral issues and highly sensitive nervous systems (autism) are being served well by horses.

The holy equine race. Trust our land whales of grace.

Check out the book or the film The Horse Boy

The Golden Alchemy of Dissonance

To dissolve dissonance within, it is wise to show it to the Light Within.

Upset is always vibratory in nature. Share the vibration.

Reveal it to Love. Do not deny/stuff away the vibration.

When you feel discordant vibration within you, let it be okay.

Don't fear it. Hug it with grace.

Surf upset fearlessly, in Great Love.

Simply don't believe it or respond to it.

It is wise to not attack inwardly or outwardly.

Simply ask the Light within you to dissolve it.

It will dissolve sooner or later. Peace will return.

Upset dissolves when we do not feed it our Light.

Light always assists when we ask for help.

(On the flip side, Light will not interfere if not invited in.)

As you practice you will discover yourself less reactive to stories.

This is called lightworking or vibrational healing.

It is a practice that helps quicken awakening.

Practice Love whenever you are upset or feeling less than peaceful.

Massaging acupressure points can also quicken a release of energy.

Adventuring with Slow Light

As a young child I knew that the speed of light was slow.

...at least what we humans call the speed of light...

When I heard about the speed of light I thought, "That's slow!"

How does a child know the speed of light is slow?

I would come to find out this is accurate.

What is faster than this light? A lot!

Can you feel this? YOU and...

The speed of the Big Bang?

The speed of the thought to separate from ONE (kind of)?
(Our mind is eternally held within a container within One.)

The radiant speed at which the cosmic container was made?

A speed way, way, way faster than the speed of light!

The Still Radiant Cosmic Container holds us safely.

A real separation wasn't possible.

Only a dream of separation occurred.

A hologram, a matrix of our mind.

(Light grants every deeply felt wish.
Be heart full with what you wish for!)

Shifting Adventures

Shift now,

shift forever.

Can you feel it?

Our Light?

I can

too.

All Life is frequency held within a Still Core.

We are pendulums of Life in a single moment.

In motion. At rest. In motion. At rest. Infinitely.

Inner~restingly, infinite speed is the same as stillness![33]

Our awareness is pure frequency. Our awareness feels and senses far differently than with what our mind calls emotion (energy-in-motion). In our veiled state, we attach all sorts of names to inner sensations of frequency, including happiness, joy and despair.

When we remove our focus from labeling our experience as good or bad, and simply accept our experience as pure awareness, we are beginning to grasp that our mind often misunderstands what is occurring within us.

As we forgive our responses to our experience and the responses of others, allowing what is to be okay, we become far less attached to stories of pain.

Listen with surrendered awareness.

Trust the flow of Life within you.

---

33   Research the work of scientists who study Light and the quantum realm.

Resonating Mountain Adventures

Our Light feels a single resonating Still Core of Light.

Light is always palpable within and all around.

~ ~ ~

Adventure with the following story…

When I climbed mountains with people who expressed belief in me, I was a more confident climber and partner.

One time I climbed Mt. Baker's Roman Wall[34] without an ice ax.

I did this only because a climbing partner insisted.

I could have said, "No way, dude." I didn't.

It felt vital to trust his trust in me.

I climbed with presence.

At first, I was nervous.

Then, I grew calmer.

Soon, I felt enlivened, aware and gently confident.

The mountain and I became deeply felt friends.

Disclaimer:

Please do not climb steep mountain terrain without an ice axe. This story is shared as a teaching tool to demonstrate how, when we are with others who express belief in us, we resonate with higher frequency. We gravitate toward trusting our abilities. Please trust the guidance of professionals and common sense when undertaking an activity.

---

34   The Mt. Baker referred to here is an active volcano located in the North Cascades of Washington State.

Remembering the Real Adventure

It cannot be stated often enough, our focus on
"not Love" blocks the Light from our awareness.

Our mind is deeply veiled to astonishing wonder.

Our ego is reluctant to surrender into the Light.

We are afraid we will lose the world.

This is why it is of value to look at the world.

If you believe this is paradise, look around you.

Listen around you. Watch the daily news. Just a bit.

Our focus on criticism, cruelty, shame and blame

blocks us to what is really real, to what is natural.

Ask your most cherished Enlightened Master.

There are quite a few, including You!

To lose a world of pain is nothing.

Trust the mighty kind heart of us all.

Together, we are re-gaining everything.

Recall, the Enlightened cannot take away
our fear, our wish to not be at peace.

Life is a free will zone to know Self/One/God or to, for a time, forget.

Forgetting our Unified Light is called fear and pain.

Adventuring with Jesus

As a kid, I fainted a lot in church. So much talk of guilt, shame and blame.

I had an on-going vision of sitting alone on a bench in a dark, dank cave.

I loved Jesus though. Jesus never speaks of guilt as real. He is very smart.

He knows our mind is veiled to our astonishing wonder. He fully transcended the dream. His fear utterly dissolved. He returned to full awareness of Source.

Our veiled mind (ego) always wants to break down, systematize and classify. This is absolutely fine in space-time. It just doesn't wake us up to what's true.

Jesus is not boo hoo. He is Divine Radiance, as are YOU!

Divine Intelligence knows exactly where to insert the Light, so the message of Unconditional Love gets through to us.

We are strangely dreaming of lots of not Wholly Love.

Jesus taught the Golden Guidance to help us wake up.

Forgive all error, He said. It's all a mistake.

See only the Light. And you will see Life.

I like this idea. Better yet, it works!

By the way, have you ever noticed…

Masters shed their bodies just like us?

We are free to choose. Others can only guide.
Jesus played his role well, transcending fear.
The Inner Light is now and always within us.

Give Everyone A Golden Heart

Give everyone a Golden Heart. Always. Trust that we are doing our best.
Be gentle inside. Communicate. Give people the benefit of the doubt.

Fear doesn't make healthy assumptions, yet this is nothing to fear. Let go of the story.
Love has nothing to do with personality or story. Go within to
remind yourself that you are safe in the Light. You are capable of
remembering Heaven now. Fear is always ungenerous, judgmental
and unkind. Forgive fear. Hug ego. We fear we are not safe.

Bring into awareness a way for you to reinforce within your
essence that if someone, including you, is feeling afraid or unkind
you stop, look within and listen within for better information.
Please take notes of Light. Focus on their Light for them.

Find the sun bow inside. Find the Golden Heart of All. Love will guide.

Even though I have mystical experiences all the time and know that this world
is an illusion coming from within my own mind, I still live here and have lots of
experiences where I feel separate and not always safe or loved or beautiful.

To help me remain present and uplift others and myself I use many techniques.
One technique is placing Love note reminders in all kinds of common places.

I write phrases and refer often to them. Here are some of these phrases. [35]

We are beautiful and really great!
Only Love is real. Trust Love always.
We are really weird. This is a-okay.
Trust kindness in all circumstances.
I am never upset for the reason I think.
In my defenselessness my safety lies.
Making a mistake is impossible.
There is nothing to fear.
We are all cherished.
I am safe right now.

---

35   Some phrases are from *A Course in Miracles*. Others feel natural for me to focus on in a given day.
Trust your intuition for what words help you shift within and for how to uplift everyone in a given moment.

Adventuring with Family Resonators

*Family relationships can give us deep clues about how active
our ego (split-mind) is and how active our Love awareness is.*

*When guilt/fear/ego gets triggered, an intense in-reaction-to may occur.
When we feel energetic dissonance within, part of us doesn't want to react.
Another part feels a pull to react defensively. Only one of these "parts" is real.*

Be a keen witness. Record the awareness of having a split-mind. Go quietly within.

*This is what awakened beings share: Do not believe
any upset is real. Trust that upset
is coming from within you, not from outside, even though an
external situation may be triggering you. Don't believe any story in the
mind yet honor the feelings. See everything as a call for Love, from
yourself or from another. What we are feeling is existential fear or guilt.
Fear is simply the part of us that feels alone/separated from.*

*We are seeking to feel safe and valuable in every
circumstance and in every moment.*

*As we recognize that all disruption is coming from within us,
we become more willing to rest and go within our Still Core.
From this state, we are more able to respond with clarity and
respect for all involved. You will know what is best. Trust
the vibration of peace, which always has everyone's best
interests at heart, even if someone needs to leave.*

In our defenselessness our safety lies.[36]

*Pure awareness is peaceful because it knows that
force is not the source of power.
Force needs energy to keep it alive. When we
become our Still Core, Light is known.*

Real power is Love's stillness.

---

36 This is a key teaching from enlightened beings and *A Course in Miracles*.

Adventuring with Colin Powell

Bring to awareness Colin Powell.

Mr. Powell has an exceptional ability to be in the fray, not of it.

His is often a voice of Light within ego (posturing) chaos.

Mr. Powell is aware that ego makes a situation rigid.
He knows Divine Intelligence is flowing. Affirming Life.
When we trust Light, it is easier for others to trust Light.

World peace is always an individual choice. Inner
peace invariably affects the whole in a helpful way.

Why is this so?

We are fundamentally a Singularity, One Pure Awareness,
temporarily appearing on the world stage in separate forms.

No one is left out of Heaven. This is impossible. Love is Wholly One.

Yet, forcing awareness of Heaven is impossible because forcing
is not Unconditional Love. Forcing is not Divinely Intelligent.
Force requires resistance. Power is the Still Core of Love.[37]

We can dream of a lack of power and radiance for a while.
Yet, we are existentially not happy not recalling what we are.
And, we know all dreams in this world eventually cease to be.

Yet, Love doesn't take away our free will to be what we are not.
We can remember we are always in Heaven in any moment.

What experience are you trusting today?

---

[37] *Power Vs Force: The Determinants of Human Behavior* by David Hawkins has some interesting bits.

Jesus and Jupiter

Volunteering is a great way to be of service and meet people in a new community. While acquainting myself with Flagstaff, Arizona, I became a volunteer at the Lowell Observatory, in their Space Theater. Lowell is renowned as the observatory where a long suspected planet was discovered. The planet was Pluto[38] (a child would name it). The Lowell is also home to the 24" Clark refractor telescope once used by N.A.S.A. astronauts and scientists to map the moon for the Apollo manned space missions.

During my volunteer nights, I learned that the planet Jupiter takes a lot of hits by space debris. (Some have made world news.) The planet Jove[39] does its best to protect to our solar system's inner planets, including Earth. Does this remind you of anyone? Jesus and Jupiter have been shown to possess a strong cosmological relationship, and Jesus and Jupiter are entirely willing to absorb hits by ego/debris because they know their Divine Radiance is real. Jupiter is a shining planet in our night sky that almost became (may yet become!) a star due to its mass, energy and ability to absorb massive impact.

A few years ago I learned that Jupiter was part of a planetary conjunction that formed the astronomically and astrologically significant Star of Bethlehem event. [40] The effect from the conjunction was identifiable by astronomers looking for anomalies. From the perspective of an earth bound gazer, Jupiter and Venus joined twice to become the brightest object in the night sky (with the exception of the moon) at an auspicious time.

The joining of masculine (Jupiter) and feminine (Venus) starlight heralded a significant event, the birth of a Divinely Radiant entity to be called Yehoshua ben Yosef, Jesus in our language. Jupiter is prominent in our night sky. Significantly prominent. Divine Intelligence knows exactly how to divinely time everything. Everything.

Our awakening is written in the cosmos.
The data is not difficult to unearth.
Yet, nothing is written in stone.

---

38 *Pluto* is now classified as a dwarf planet.
39 *Jupiter* or *Jove* is the Roman king of the gods, equivalent of Zeus in Greek mythology.
40 Based on remarkable research by Frederick A. Larson (bethlehemstar.org).
Jesus' given name is debated as Yeshua, Yehoshua, Jeshua.

Love's Radiant Engineering

It's great to explore the world for clues of our dreaming state.

Love's patterns in nature and the cosmos are leading us to go within.

Scientists are discovering the holographic engineering of Divine Intelligence.

Source can always be known. Let go of shame and blame. Free the mind.

Be aware that no human-made system,
no worldly ingenuity, will wake us up.
Explore the word itself: in genuine.

Cleverness and originality is mightily used.
Yet, babies and grown-ups cry out in pain.
This world is, categorically, not a real thing.

It is taking awhile for us to trust the Inner Light of Love.
We simply cannot wake up while looking outside ourselves.
It is a scientific impossibility. Yet, looking outside is giving us clues.
Evidence that we rest within Home in this very instant is everywhere.
Animals perceive far more both of the dreaming state and of paradise.

Awakening is always an inner journey.

Forgive the whole world's errors.

Forgive all wild dreams.

Love with Might.

Trust Light.

Love's Creation

Love did not create a world of pain and suffering.
Love created Heaven where all is known as One.

When we chose to veil our awareness of Oneness, we were Love.

We remain Love. We remain in Heaven.

Love is not a person. Love is not a thing. Love is everything and beyond thing.

Our world of grief, our world of horrors, our world of unsharing, is a false place.
This world is not real. Our unkindness and our disregard for Life masks Heaven.

As we Love, as we brighten our awareness, as we dance and draw together,
we are waking up from an ancient sleep. Enlightened Love from beyond
the veils in our own mind constantly reach toward us from within us.

Bring into your mind the kind and gentle times in your life.
Bring into your mind the acts of grace that you have faced.
Bring into mind dreams unattained. These are gifts of Life.

When we pursue dreams in amnesia we
keep Heaven veiled from our awareness.

The goal is not to stay asleep/in pain.
The goal is to illuminate/remember.

When we awaken from dreams,
we create as we were created,
with full awareness of our Divinity,
with full awareness of our Unity.

Trust Love's guidance as you move through your moments.
Here in the dream we are guided perfectly for our awakening.
While we may still eat and sleep and dream awhile, we are safe.

Now is Close to Eternity

"Now" is the closest we can get to eternity in time.[41]

Right NOW you are exquisite radiance.
Can you feel this? Know this is true for all.

If you have a worry, a grief or a fear on your mind,
give it to Love. Place it into the core of your Being.
Place all needs into Light's grace. The Light will
guide you perfectly for how to meet any need.

You will make decisions in your life.
Make decisions with the faith of Life.
Ask if your decision serves the whole.

If you make a choice that feels at first hurtful to an other,
yet you make it with a full heart of Love for all, it is fine.
The perfect flow will always result. We are not amiss.
Unanswered prayer or a painful goodbye is often a gift.

Love is often unrecognized.
Love feels our true prayers.

True prayer is to awaken to realize
we never left Heaven's embrace.

We are Divine Radiance.

We are Light.

We are unmistakable Grace.

---

41   Long asserted by spiritualists and long proved by science, *time is an illusion.* Divine Intelligence/ God/the Absolute/Love can only communicate with us *in the moment* since the eternal "Now" is all that exists.

Why We Fear Waking Up

If you are a Star Trek fan or scientifically inclined, imagine a warp bubble.
This is a perfect metaphor (not a metaphor!) for our dream of separation.

Yesterday I switched on the television.
Star Trek: The Next Generation was showing.
Dr. Beverly Crusher became caught in a warp bubble
made by her son Wesley's experiment. (We are that Son.)

It was the perfect episode to watch while writing The Mix Up.
(Divine Intelligence always has a way of getting through.)
Beverly was frightened that her world was dissolving.
She didn't know that she was in a warp bubble
and that paradise lay beyond her deep fear.

This is exactly why we are so reluctant to trust Love.
We are afraid that the world in our mind will dissolve.
We do not realize our own thoughts block our Light.

Our belief in stories of this world veils our awareness of peace.
Yet, often, our psyche relaxes only enough to recognize this in
our more painful moments, when we are crying out for mercy.
When we, or our friends, are tired of ancient repeating stories.

Set aside distractions and addictions that mask and numb.
Use your moments to go deeply within. Ask for Light.
Overlook when you or another forgets to go within.

True humility is surrendering ego stories and
trusting everyone's Light, including our own.

Ask to know the Truth.

Relax within.

You will marvel.

Apply and Trust Love's Oxygen Mask

*We are familiar with the aircraft safety protocol,
"Please place the oxygen mask over your
own face and nose before assisting others."*

*Radiant self-care is vital to group care.
If we cannot breathe, we cannot help.*

*Nobel prize winning economist, mathematician and Princeton scholar John Nash,
Jr. came to discover that self-care and group care are equally essential via his
contemplations and calculations and his journey into paranoid schizophrenia.*[42]

Why trust Love?

*Our awareness is continually seeking a compass bearing, an attunement.
It is asking for data from within. It is asking, "Shall we trust fear/illusion/ego/
me or Light/unity?" As we tune our loving intention to our Still Core (apply
Love's oxygen mask) during an upset, the upset will naturally pass away. It
will dissolve. This is science. The reason an upset will pass away is simple. It
is not real. All fear, guilt and upset is an illusion of dissonance coming from
deep within, even though ego may point to a story claiming the opposite.*

*It is important to note that fear may
increase the closer we get to the Light.
Be sure to always trust Love to guide.*

We are all on the same team. Apply your radiant oxygen mask.

---

42   The word *schizophrenia* literally means *split-mind*. We all have a split/veiled-mind, which is our
choice to trust the illusion of fear/separation/belief in unworthiness. The split-mind manifests more
dramatically within individuals who don't remember everyone's Light. As we trust Love, we are
enlightening from the split state.

Bring a CapCom Onboard

In the world of U.S. human space exploration and communication there is an extraordinary position called a Capsule Communicator, CapCom for short. The CapCom is the only individual on the ground, on the earth, that has voice communication with crew operating a spaceship. This single line of communication ensures that there is no confusion about what is being shared. The CapCom receives information from the Flight Director, who is receiving data from many individual sources. A Flight Director makes assessments based on his or her overall awareness of data. This Flight Director then feeds information for the astronauts through the CapCom.

A CapCom is usually an astronaut, a person who knows exactly what it feels like to be in the hot seat and why a calm demeanor and clear communication is vital. They are also familiar intimately with many operations. Rent the film Apollo 13 and watch closely for who holds the position of CapCom. Notice how the CapCom is the only person talking with the ship's crew and how profoundly calmly he speaks no matter what is occurring within or around. Astronauts are deeply aware of their role as an astronaut and also regarding spaceship operations and ground operations. They know to the core that mission success and crew survival depends on their ability to focus calmly on what matters most in any moment. Holding a calm, informed presence is fundamental.

If you have a challenge in your life where you are feeling disrespected, or where you are not responding to those around with love and respect, forgive yourself and forgive the other. Trust that neither of you feels safe, cherished and seen. Ego is always fighting for survival because it is scared. Hug ego. It has forgotten it never left the Light of Being.

If you find yourself in a bind of ego mind, ask a trusted friend or colleague if they would serve as your CapCom. Ask if they would listen to information you feel is vital to convey to another, and ask if they would listen to information the other feels vital to convey to you. Ask if they might serve as a capsule-communicator-of-mutual-respect so that all feel valued. Let go of assumption and expectation. Trust your own goodwill and the goodwill of others, even if feels excruciating at first. CapComs serve the Light of Truth.

Our Amnesia Mind Wants Odds and Trusts Fear

Fear wants to know, "Will (fill in the blank) succeed?"

Our heart doesn't look for odds. It knows only Love is real.

Love is fail-safe. Love transcends. Love is quantum holy prayer.

(Bring to mind Apollo 13.[43] Odds did not cause the astronauts return. The crew survived because they believed they would, and they had prepared to accomplish all tasks side-by-side with many helpers.)

We are attempting to awaken from an ancient painful dream.

Angels weep that we do not see what we really are. Golden.

Do you feel safe in this world of "to do" lists, crazy distractions, bills, etc.?

Be honest. Look around. Look inside. How safe do you feel, really?

Our Light is the realm of miracles. Love transcends physical laws.

Light compresses and expands in ways we do not fully understand.

Fear has its lowly, stuck limits. Heaven's power does not have limits.

Mayhem is only possible within a dream of mind.

We know the body shifts. This is a physical fact.

The Truth of You never does. Our Soul is eternal.

If we keep our mind locked in guilt and hate, we experience the effects.

When we free our mind and trust in peace, we experience our True Nature.

---

43 Multiple catastrophic failures occurred on the Apollo 13 spacecraft. When one looks only at the systemic failures and the data it becomes obvious that far more was required to bring the men home than scientific knowledge. It was utterly impossible, by the data, that they lived and to return to earth. Many radiant hearts trusted enough to slow down and make wise decisions. We stood vigil and vibrated them home.

A Successful "Failure"

Wowsa! Have we ever been successful or what!

And, do we ever know what failure feels like!

Thing is, failure only happens in dreams.

We are getting' it! We are bringin' it!

We are bringing Light back to memory.

Each time we trust Love, even when we

feel like we've failed, we are bringin' it!

In fact, it is in our moments that feel

hard that we're most willing

to remember our Light.

When in pain we often

journey deep inside.

Next time you are crying out in pain, or holding pain within, afraid to feel it, offer it to the Light. Offer your upset to Source. Become your own CapCom.

Adventuring with Oil

*Our focus around oil and all perceived need
in this world is a grand forgiveness opportunity.*

*If we believe for a moment that we are not intimately connected with
every aspect of this world, human and otherwise, we are deeply asleep.*

*What we always want to look for in any circumstance is the inner conflict.
Ask your Light to feel into inner conflict. Your heart will guide you well
in this. Our awareness is deeply aware of our fundamental unity. When
we take and use without honoring all life, our awareness, our being,
feels this conflict. Our ego stuffs away its inner conflict. Look.*

*We are in conflict because we are terrified. This is cause for Love's compassion!
In Truth, we are not terrified of not having oil. We are terrified of not being safe.
Existentially safe. This fear causes us to project and to not listen to our intuition. Oil is
a profound gift in so many ways. Our inner and outer battles around oil are helping
all wake up. We know something isn't quite right in Who-What-Whereville. As we stuff
away what is occurring within us we block our access to Divine Intelligence to help
us. Light/Divine Intelligence, always offers helpful information for working out life-
affirming collaborations. Look within to see. Tune deeply within. Do not judge our
predicament or players who appear to be more blatantly disregarding the whole
than we believe we are. We are fundamentally a unified awareness. The whole
is never separate from the whole. We are One. Separateness is fundamentally an
illusion. This is a fact long proved by scientific data and long asserted by our most
well known teachers, those who have enlightened. No one can force another to
compromise his/her own enlightened integrity, regardless of external circumstances.
We are free. Even those who are subject to horrific external circumstances are
capable of tuning into their true nature. The world is filled with these stories. Few
who are using oil in our world are being physically forced to do so. Oil is a gift.
Everything is a gift. When we criticize, blame and shame we are not existentially
happy. Wisdom is to let go of guilt for the past. It is not real. Look to Light for solutions.*

Share your upsets with the Light.

Call upon Love for all peoples.

Gather as One and heartstorm.

A Lake of Light

I often hike around a tiny, beautiful
lake that is home to many bird species.

The walks bring often the work of Itzak Bentov to mind.
Bentov wrote brilliantly on the fundamental unity of life.
For example, we are immersed within fields of frequency.
Whenever we make the smallest of movements, a sound
wave is generated that travels to the end of the universe.
Wow we! How can we make the movements of peace?

Our ego only thinks that it is not connected to others and to everyone
and everything. Our heart feels intimately our fundamental connection.

The subtle and gross fields that we are immersed within and being affected
by are ONEdrous to contemplate. Truly, some would go so far as to say our
consciousness creates these fields. This is rather quite accurate information!

Deeply felt thoughts are motion. They are Love-in-action.
Felt-thoughts are quantum vibratory creators. They exist.
For an inkling, smile! Extend your "whee!" side to side.
How do you feel inside? Ponder how you respond to the
adventure of Life when you are smiling versus moaning.

Daily Ten-Minute Miracle-Working Adventure
As you practice, remain open hearted and focused on golden or sun bow Light.

For the first five minutes
Bring into your awareness someone you love dearly. Gently close
your eyes, tune your heart and move into a vibration of gratitude
for this person. See them in an exquisite sphere of golden sun bow
Light. Do not enter the sphere. Simply hold lovely space.

For the next five minutes
Repeat this exercise with someone whose presence feels somewhat
uncomfortable or unpleasant for you. Let whatever comes be okay.

Repeat this practice, or create your own, as needed.

Love Satellites

Satellites we kind of are.

Divinely Intelligent devices.

We float, broadcast and receive signals.

Static and coherent at once.

Always. In eternity.

Static blocks the reception of Coherent Light,

the harmonic frequencies of Divine Intelligence.

Life is oscillating within a Still Radiant Container.
We are, quite literally, fields of radiant (star) Light.
Our "frequency bodies" feel and sense far more
intensely than by what mind calls emotion.
Emotion is energy-is-motion. Energy is dense
frequency. Energy, like body, is temporary.[44]

Energy is not eternal. It shifts. It dances.
Like body, energy is a tool for us to play.
Frequency sensations offer information.
We are Light oscillating in the Absolute.

Nervous systems are highly attuned to the Light

Feel into your Radiant Light. It is here!

---

44 This fact regarding energy's changeable/non-eternal nature is well described in *A Course in Miracles* and in science. Energy is part of a matrix of creative potential that allows us to manifest and experience form (material objects with boundaries and relative mass), including our dense physical form and light body forms, such as astral or etheric bodies, which are also contained within our collective hologram. The astral and etheric are no more permanent than this dense physical world. Many teachers share of the holographic/mind nature of the universe. Check out the research of Itzak Bentov and many others.

A Spark of Light Split[45]

Every Spark of Light (soul) born into this world has their Divine Memory partly veiled. We came to assist a strange thought in our mind to end, the thought to be separate from Divine Intelligence. This curious thought to separate led to a fragmentation in our mind, a fragmentation that is temporary. A holographic world was created by Love.

We have an innate sense of our eternal Radiant Divine nature, our perfection and our beauty, wholeness and unity with all life. We feel this in our Still Radiant Core. Yet, due to self-inflicted trauma in our mind, we are deeply afraid that we are unworthy, alone and broken and/or that others are. This split/veiled or dual-minded circumstance (think of DNA that is turned-off) occurred in an instant, during a cosmic wish for everything to be different than it was. A wish to "not Know Thyself."[46] (There are many ways our Cosmic Mind's fragmentation/separation event is described in various spiritual traditions.).

The splitting caused a deep trauma within our mind. This is what we feel when we are upset. We feel alone and broken, shattered. What is fundamentally One cannot be unOne, or undone. Beyond all shattering sensations inside, exist joy and peace.

As we listen within, the Light is singing us home. Light can be felt.

Trust your heart's joyful knowing and peace.

Waking up from what we are not is inevitable.

Celebrate everything!

We are a miracle of Light.

Help a child feel their Light.

---

45   The split-minded state is astonishingly well described in *A Course in Miracles* and in many traditions. Some call our present *amnesia of paradise* a dreamtime. We also call it having a veiled or split-mind. Words are not important. The fact is that our curious thought to separate caused a side effect. We unintentionally forgot what we are. Now we are illuminating to the fact that we never left Home. We rest safely in Love.

46   *Holy Spirit's Interpretation of the New Testament* is a beautiful sharing on this subject.

The Zone

Have you felt it?

The zone?

Athletes speak of it. We all know it.

When we're in the zone we're unstoppable.

I'm not usually a football viewer, but today I watched with Sue,
a sister of heart who loves the sport. So fun to enjoy another's joy!

These Holy Beings love what they do. They love having and
being "ahponements," as a quite young friend says.
("Ahponements" is her way of saying opponents.)
These dudes love to risk being pushed and tackled.
I love to say tightly hugged which cracks up Sue.

We set our vision on a Seattle Seahawks/New Orleans match. We saw
Divine Intelligence in the zone in the form of a Seattle Seahawks player
who ran 67 yards for a touchdown. This player was utterly unstoppable,
breaking through multiple aggressive hugging attempts. Our jaws
dropped at his finesse. At one point, with what looked like barely a finger
push, this radiant Knight of Light sent an attempted hugger flying.

In this world, without "ahponements," many of our games would not play.
(I love the likeness to the word atonement—at-one-ment—Oneness.)

When we see our "ahponements" as One with us, like the
warriors of old knew to be true, we are almost awake.

You are Divine Intelligence in the Zone.

Stories about what happens when we encounter our resistance/fear and trust Love:

Tooth Fairy (2010) a delightful film about a hockey player and his resistance
Believe in Me (2006) amazing film about a girls' basketball coach in 1964

Or, check out the book Sacred Hoops, by Phil Jackson, former
Head Coach of the Chicago Bulls and the Los Angeles Lakers

Competition and Collaboration

Competition is a concept of our deeply veiled mind.
Mind holds a deep fear. This is helpful to recognize.
Fear is a concern for bodily and existential survival.
Ego often believes it must compete to Live, to exist.

Nothing could be further from Truth.

Fear is Love unrecognized. Hug your fear.

Our courage to trust Love is enormous.

Remember situations where you gave collaboratively
and unconditionally even though you didn't need to.

What happened in your trust, even if you were afraid?

Seek out and feel into the stories of those who offer grace.
The heart does not see competition. Only Love is known.
How many stories must be told where Love was shown?
It is a misunderstanding that there is not enough Life.
We mis-create illusions when we are ungenerous.
There are infinite ways to ensure needs are met.

Collaboration is stunningly effective for reducing fear/ego identification.
(Check out the story of Apollo 13 and the millions of other stories out here.)

It is untrue that we are separate. This is full-on fact.
We mis-create when we promote competition.
Yet, we are not to fight competition.
Oh nope, nope, nopey, nope.
Fighting keeps illusion alive.
Painful dreams will remain.

Simply Love away all fear.

Trusting Apollo 13's Miracle

Many of us old folk remember the story of Apollo 13, the moon mission that experienced multiple catastrophic failures prior to reaching the moon. Without round-the-clock efforts of scores of individuals tuning into Divine Intelligence, and the prayers of millions around the globe, three calm and courageous astronauts would not have returned from space.

I used to manage and help design websites for two radiant companies. On several occasions, by deeply contemplating a glitch, we would have an insight that provided a simple solution rather than a major overhaul.

It is often helpful to have a variety of people working on a circumstance that may appear troublesome. Those closest and excellently capable of designing system elements may not see something an "uneducated" bystander solves instantly simply by considering an alternative angle or the bigger picture.

Bring to heart when you received an insight from deep within.

We access Divine Intelligence in innumerable ways.

When collaborating and enjoying our projects and another's company, it is astounding what comes.

What is your Apollo 13 miracle?

Signs from the Great Healer

Love is the Healer.

*There is a wondrous story by the scribe of A Course
in Miracles. Dr. Helen Schucman was
a professor of medical psychology at Columbia University's
College of Physicians and Surgeons. Her area of expertise
prior to scribing A Course in Miracles? The split-mind.*

Helen experienced astounding dreams and revelation. Here is one of her dreams:[47] She was standing in a boat floating down a calm, straight canal. A thought came to her, "I wonder if there is buried treasure. I shouldn't be surprised if there were." Then, she says, "I noticed a long pole with a large hook on the end lying in the boat. 'Just the thing!' I thought, dropping the hook into the water and reaching the pole down as far as I could. The hook caught something heavy, and I raised it with difficulty. It was an ancient treasure chest. There was nothing in the chest but a large black book. On the spine one word was written in gold, 'Aesculapius.' The word was familiar, but I could not remember what it meant. When I looked it up, I found that it was the name of the Greek god of healing." Helen said she saw the same black book a few nights later in another dream. She said, "This time there was a string of pearls around it." Interesting.

This is a fascinating dream for many reasons. We all have heard of December 21, 2012, a pivotal date signaling of an Age of Enlightenment.[48] We are shifting from the emotional (watery) Piscean Age to the Light (air) Aquarian Age. (Aquarius is an air sign, not a water sign.) This shift into enlightenment is an inner shift. Note Helen reaching into water. Water is the symbol of emotion. She brought the ancient book into the Light (air). Pisces is the ancient sign of the fish symbolizing humanity. In ancient art we are portrayed in a net (of mind). Fish/we swim in water, dense substance, plasma, mind. In other words, we are caught in a net or matrix of emotional experience. The sign of the Age of Light is Aquarius, an air sign associated with delivery, the water bearer no less!

---

47   This documentary appears on YouTube. First link: http://www.youtube.com/watch?v=5wvY9KkOXUY Helen's description of the dream with the chest bearing the name Aesculapius appears in Segment #2.

48   Famous intuitive Edgar Cayce describes this time now as the Age of Purity (edgarcayce.org).

For those familiar with astronomy and astrology, it is ancient knowledge that there are actually thirteen, not twelve, constellations along the elliptic through which our superb solar system moves.[49] This is astronomically significant. It is also significant to note the relationship of thirteen to a great teacher of Light. Jesus plus twelve disciples equals thirteen.[50] Jesus delivered of the message of our Radiant Light as He dissolved the veils in His own mind. The story of our falling deeply asleep, and our awakening, is written in the cosmos. The thirteenth constellation is called Ophiucus. This constellation is associated with Aesculapius, the Healer, the Christ. (Recall Helen's dream and her subsequent recording of A Course in Miracles.) Another association with Ophiucus is the Serpent Holder, an ancient symbol for physician/healer/healed. Ophiucus touches the elliptic[51] for as long as Scorpio. Notably, this constellation was incorporated in ancient science, including the work of mystic/scientist/artist Leonardo Di Vinci. On December 21, 2012, the sun will be aligned with the center of our Milky Way Galaxy in the constellation of Ophiucus (Aesculapius/Christ), the healed, the illuminated.

As this date approaches, ego wants to extend toward doom and gloom and body identification. It says, "If my body dies. I might die too. I am deeply afraid for me." Divine Intelligence is sharing is that we never left Heaven. We never left perfection.

We are always seeing the effects of our awakening within the world and within the cosmos because they are actually within us, within our Pure Awareness. They are not external to us. We can look to any number of teachings by beings that confirm this.

Divinely Intelligent patterns in the cosmos are evidence of awareness. So many have looked to the stars, to the world around us, to the world within us, trying to figure out what is up. We inquire, "Why do we suffer? Why do we not remember what we are and where we come from?"

These are reasonable questions with reasonable answers.

Do we have infinite overwhelming conundrums in this world, or a simple misunderstanding?

---

49 I learned of Ophiucus while volunteering at the Lowell Observatory in Flagstaff, Arizona. I was thunderstruck. I knew to research this circumstance. I had not yet learned of Helen's dream.
50 There is much wonder to be explored in the ancient science of sacred geometry.
51 The elliptic is the circle formed by the earth's yearly circling/orbiting of our local star, the sun.

Consider Occam's Razar:

*The simplest explanation
is usually the right one.*

Be Aware

*Just like our earthly transition from dark to light,
it may seem to get very dark before the dawn.
This is not because waking up is hard.
This is because our ego is wacky.*

The Human Antenna

Most of us cannot remember much of our Source.

An interesting case of amnesia we might say.

We have not been left without exceptional tools to tune in to our Source.

The ancients understood, and contemporary scientists are aware, that the human form (and all life) serves as highly refined antenna. Our heart and brain are receivers and amplifiers of high frequency, harmonics, vibration, in essence Source thoughts.

As we connect more fully within to our physical tools and harmonic capability, we are experiencing awakening effects.

The cosmos and all life, including our human form, is either tuned to Divine Intelligence or to static (illusion/fear) in any given moment. Static is much more dense and far slower than Source/God-speed.

Humanity is learning how to listen, and when two or more gather, the result is astounding.

Strive to hold your awareness in Radiant Light.

A mind in the Light does miraculous science. A mind in the Light designs healthy systems.

A mind in the Light wakes up to wonder.

The Sight and Certainty of Love

Only our amnesia of our golden radiance leads to suffering.

*We are unspeakably loved and cherished. Only we judge
anything as less than perfect, keeping vile in our mind alive.
All the while, our Inner Light radiance remains the same.*

*I just re-watched a film (and loved the book by the same name) that affected
me profoundly many, many years ago. The Last Temptation of Christ is stunningly
clear about our mind's dilemma. Jesus was willing to know—beyond his fear and
temporary amnesia—that only Love, that only Divine Intelligence, is real and is
found within—the only place it has ever been. I can see my own fear coming
up around sharing more publicly in the world knowing that unkind words might
come my way. My fear of being treated unkindly remains a bit alive. This is why
many shy from the public eye. Legions of beings are aware of our split-minded/
dreaming state and are working under the radar. In Truth, all are working in
this way. We are all on the exact same adventure—dissolving fear in our own
mind. We all rotate in and out taking our own heat to dissolve our fear, even if
our own mind, our own amnesia, gives us a run. We're all doing dashingly!*

*Love's Radiance never hurts or burns. Fire and heat are worldly things.
The ego always wants to call another wrong for sharing the message of
Love. Look where fear sent Jesus' body. Ego always hates Love. That's
its job. This is why we must hug our ego/fear, and ask Love to help us
through. The world is not real. It's coming from our own mind.*

In you are inclined, check out the book or the film The Last Temptation of Christ.

No Enemies

I watched a movie again recently that impacted me deeply as a child.

It is called Against a Crooked Sky.

Its message is for the wildly brave warrior within.

We are brave. Know it well.

What are you certain of?

What would you die for?

When we would die for family or friends, we are learning.

When we would die for "an enemy," we are no longer mixed up.

*When we know death and enemies are fallacy only ego believes,
we are long past the need for books or teachers or all the world.*

We have illuminated.

*The teaching to Love your enemies is deeply wise. As we Love our enemies
we come to recognize we have no enemies. We are not bodies. We are not
personalities. We are Divine Radiance. We are One Light with an intense case of
forgetting. Physical bodies break down quickly or eventually. Form is a temporary
vehicle for Spirit. What Jesus was sharing, and profoundly well modeled, is to
go within to the Light, especially when aggression or unkindness appears to
be coming toward you or from within you. These are powerful moments for
seeking the Light. Imagine being Jesus. He knew He was not a body. He felt
no pain. He did not die. He said, "You will do these things and greater."*

Divine Intelligence knew what Jesus was sharing would take "time" to sink in.

Bring to heart a story of when you saw the fear in another and forgave.

Shelter, Water, Fire, Food

I once took the Tracker School's Standard Course.
This is a wilderness awareness training based on
teachings of well-known tracker Tom Brown, Jr.
His teacher was a Native American shaman.

Tom and his faculty taught us the
Sacred Four: Shelter, Water, Fire, Food

In a physical survival situation, this is the optimal order
for what needs to be done to support the body's survival.

It is imperative to protect the body's heat. Find or make a shelter.
It is imperative to drink water. As a general rule, a body
cannot go for more than three days without water.
Fire keeps the body warm and curious animals at bay.
A body, it is said, can survive up to three weeks without food.
One might grow quite weak going for that long. Find food.

The Inner Journey is also
Shelter, Water, Fire, Food

We thrive when we are sheltered in the Light Within.

Research lives of masters, saints and other folks.

Eat, drink and warm yourself within.

Trust the Light.

It restores our awareness of Life.

Situational "Glowareness"

Look for the radiant glow.

In everything.

It is here.

In outdoor environments, family environments and in all environments it is wise to be aware of what is occurring within and around you.

Trust that all is well and that everyone is doing their best.

How might you help others feel more comfortable?

What would add joy and peace to your space?

Life and joy are meant to be synonymous.

The awake believe that Life is beautiful.

Life glows with wonder and glee. Now.

In remote, unforgiving outdoor settings, remaining alive, let alone comfortable, depends on situational awareness.

Happy, peaceful adventure travelers trust the inner silence, so the world around is felt.

When Life feels less than comfortable, how might you shift your awareness within to become more aware of what is around?

Extend Love to the Uncomfortable

Fearless Love comforts the fearful.

In our world, sometimes it's an adventure to feel fearlessly loving.
Other times it is astonishingly easy, like when a child is in pain.
Everything else vanishes. What matters most floats to the summit.

I spend time with a little guy who knows a lot about medical care.
He was born with a severely asthmatic condition and allergies.
He spent his first years sleeping in the hospital as often as out of it.

A few days ago, when I picked him up from school, he had
two very sore looking eyes. It was painful just looking at them.

When Mom decided to take him to a 24-hour care center,
we brought along plenty of drawing paper and pencils
and a favorite book, Ted Andrew's Animal Speak.
We sketch animals from this wondrous book.

As he was showered with attention,
there was only joy in this child.

You deserve to be cherished here.

You are cherished by Divine Intelligence.

Can you feel it? Explore your inner wellbeing.

And for an added boost, check out this procedure:
Our telepathic capabilities are still fairly well veiled here.
Let another know what helps you feel safe and comfortable.

Saving Money

*Conflict is expensive. Conflict impacts minds and bodies and
the bodies and minds of our children, families, communities,
businesses, nations, animals and the ecosystem.*

Trusting conflict delays awakening and costs a lot of money and grief.

*By relaxing into the awareness of peace and Perfect Love, we naturally
improve our mental, emotional and physical balance. The manner in
which we relate in the world opens us to expanded creative flow.*

*As we honor and affirm our Inner Light and its wisdom and
honor and affirm the Inner Light of others and their wisdom,
we naturally affect the world in helpful ways, and
save ourselves thousands of years of painful learning.*

*Belief is wondrous but not necessary.[52]
Belief comes through active practice.
Peace of mind and heart helps heal
the world effortlessly and joyfully.*

It is the Divine Science of Love.

Seek deep within your heart's core.

Ask yourself what really matters, just for today.

Is there a way to uplift yourself or another in pain?

How can you remember your radiance, just for today?

Share your play.

---

52   This information is fact-based so it works. As we practice loving, kindness and honoring self, others
and all life, we quicken our awakening. *A Course in Miracles* is very clear on this fact, as is Jesus and
many other teachers. This is why Love is taught the world over. As we trust Love, the veils in our mind
dissolve.

Adventuring with Credit

Give yourself and others credit.
Trust everyone in your heart,
even if they don't trust you.

Use common sense in the world. If you feel intuitively
a need to protect, do this from Love rather than fear.
Hold within the knowing that those who do not respect
others are in deep self-hate. As we hold a loving space
of Light we all may begin to feel our shared radiance.

Set up everyone for success.

No matter what.

Forget personality
and our preference.

Trust our Radiant Light.

This reminds us that we are safe.

This reminds us of an Ancient, Eternal Home.

Journey with what happens when you uplift children and grown-ups regardless
of how you are feeling and regardless of how your ego feels treated. Gently
disregard stories in your mind (or theirs) that want to defend, criticize, blame,
shame or fear anything at all. We are not our stories or our circumstances. We
are Light. Trust the glow of Light in you and others, even when it feels hard.
Refrain from allowing defensive or critical thoughts to fester, let alone to be
shared out loud. Give feelings straight away to the Light. Allow sensations of
upset to gently pass through unbelieved. Ride the surf wave into peace.

When at rest, ask deep inside for what feels best.

Adventure with Laundry Mountain

Next time you're contemplating a task that needs to be done, close your eyes. Bring it into your heart and mold it into the world's greatest adventure. Breathe into your dread of scaling this task-full steep peak—without a stabilizing rope to grope no less! Feel the sheer exposure below you. The stark intensity of the looming summit, a summit you're no longer sure you even sure you want to visit. After all, you think, "Who really needs clean clothes. Lots of happy people aren't all that clean." An eagle screeches past you. You tremble, raw with terror. Utterly present. Utterly frozen. You close your eyes and draw a deep breath. You exhale. You remind yourself deep within that this is something you want to do. Of all the ways you could chose to spend time, this is what you chose. You remember that no one else can choose clean clothes for you. You are free to be clean or dirty. You soon find yourself moving in to a space within that is deeper than you have ever gone before. You are fascinated. You hold your awareness here. Curious. Mindless. Empty. Still. Eventually you draw another breath and gently open your eyes. What unfolds before you is astonishing. You see a clear route up Laundry Mountain, a perfect line that you are certain was not there before your experience into your Still Radiant Laundering Core. Moreover, there is not a wisp of doubt in your mind about your ability to scale this line up the pile. Bring earth, air, fire and water into your laundry. You feel the textures of fabric against your skin. In their purest form, you remember how they come from the earth. You imagine the dryer's heat evaporating water particles from your wet attire. Gaze at the rush of water into the washtub. Thank those who invented our splendid laundering system. Climbing Laundry Mountain used to take us longer. Feel gratitude for warm apparel when it's cold outside. Feel the joy in slipping into your favorite t-shirt for a warm day's hike. Feel into the scent of your clothes as they are removed from the slow fire.

You get the adventuring picture.

Who made the "This isn't fun" rule anyway? Oh yeah, nobody!

Fire Making Reveals Radiance

I just had my nose buried in my dog's fur.

Simon smells like a campfire.

I love campfires.

Fire making skills come in handy in some worldly situations.

Let's adventure with fire making as a metaphor to transcend our veiled state of not always remembering our Loving Warm Inner Light.

Fires need the following:

A Safe Place to Build
*Ideally, a fire is constructed and contained within safe boundaries.
It is vital to be aware of your environment within and around you.
If we're not feeling safe within ourselves or in our environment,
it becomes fear more adventurous to ignite the Light within.*

Fuel
*Material is needed to construct a fire: tinder, wood and a safe container.
If you're not feeling good about your material it's hard to fuel your Light.*

Ignition
*A fire needs spark…to be lit with a match, lighter, flint and steel, friction, etc.
To discover your Inner Light, ignite a willingness to trust what's radiant within.*

Enter your Still Radiant Core.

Transcend all Inner Light dimmers.

Dolphins, Porpoises and Whales

Cetaceans and all of nature's creatures are highly attuned to Divine Intelligence.

Dolphins know how to naturally support their physical form and consciousness. In fact, dolphins are conscious breathers. They must move quickly after taking a breath so they don't fall asleep and drown. It is said the consciousness of dolphins, whales, porpoises and elephants is vibrating higher than humans. Their awareness, like ours, is Light. It is not from this world. Native traditions speak of the celestial origins of dolphins and whales.

We all tune into the same Light/Divine Intelligence.

All animals and all particles help us do this.

Trust your own Divine Intelligence to guide you into wonder.

Let go of thoughts and beliefs that weigh you down.

You will receive information like crazy!

Avalanching Adventure

I spent some months in Alaska managing a facility for a mountain climbing school. As a benefit, I was able to attend an alpine climbing course on the South Fork of the Kahiltna Glacier, an entry point for climbers attempting Denali/Mt. McKinley and other local peaks. While I'd done some climbing in the North Cascades of Washington State, a glorious and glacier clad range, nothing prepared me for the scale of the Alaska Range. It's big. Really big. Heart thumping, mouth watering, pantaloon peeing BIG.

After days spent skill building, we were heading for the summit of a nearby peak. I was on the first rope team behind the rope leader who was an instructor. Nearing the summit we spied a colossal avalanche across the way.

Our instructor was very clear there was no way the avalanche could reach us. I trusted his confidence.

We'd been witnessing avalanches all week from our base camp. Avalanches are so natural in this environment after awhile I had to remind myself to look at them. It is funny how mind so easily dismisses the astonishing when it is called normal.

On this climbing day the avalanche across the way was on an extraordinarily massive scale. It was ginormous and mightily racing across the valley floor, We were perched high on its left flank, searching furiously for...cameras.

Lacking our instructor's calm assurance, I may have been highly concerned. I may have been afraid to not be afraid. Yet, with incomprehensibly destructive forces nearby, we were in the Light, standing calmly in sparkling avalanche dust.

Divine Intelligence is aware. Ego fears and then it feels guilty for its fear, which muddles our ability to tune into the Divine Intelligence that guides us from within.

Rest calmly within even if you are running away. Respond as peace.

You will know just what do to when worldly avalanches come.

Call upon powerful memories of when you did not panic.

You Can Do Anything

For those who wish to end pain and suffering for all time,
it is wise to remember we can do anything we set our heart to.

Trust your heart's calling in this world.
We are here for a time after all.
Decisions will be made.
Choose heart-fully.

Because this world is not paradise for all, the inner questions become:

How will (fill in the blank) help unveil my mind to the astonishing
wonder that we are and that we are always immersed within?

How will (fill in the blank) help me remember
Our Light and Our Divine Intelligence?

Follow your heart song.

Help others follow theirs.

Easily forgive everyone's errors.

As we trust the Light and Heart Song of all,

letting go of all strange errors of fright,

we awaken with grace in the Light.

Rockin' in the truly free world!

We are glowing bright into it!

What is Love?

Love assumes the best and trusts the rest.

Bring to mind a story of someone who looks like
they have made a few or many mistakes in their life.

Remove all judgment for this individual from your mind.
(Know, as you do this asking, you are being released also.)

Have you ever felt like you needed a good friend?
Have you ever felt like the world is a strange place
where you find yourself compromising your values?

When we recognize our human choices as a call for Love,
forgiving choices we wish could be taken back is easy.

As we bless and honor all our calls for Love,
no matter how horrific or strange they seem,
we help everyone awaken to our true nature.

Is there someone in your world who may feel
unworthy, lost or too timid to ask for Love?

How can we help each other feel safe and worthy?

Loving helps us all enlighten a whole lot faster.

Divinely Intelligent Resources

We share the same Divine Intelligence.

We are in constant communication with Light.

This is fact, whether we are in Love or in fear.

Here are some Divine feeling adventures:

***August Rush**, a wondrous film story that explores the value of trust and of listening*

***Hubble Space Telescope** website, hubblesite.org*

***Temple Grandin**, a film based on the life of an autistic prodigy*

***From Atom to Cosmos**, a documentary on Itzak Bentov's work*

*HeartMath website, **heartmath.org** HeartMath conducts and publishes research*

***The Divine Matrix** and other books by Gregg Braden*

***Peaceful Warrior**, a film based on the life of Dan Millman*

***Apollo 13**, a miracle about the return of stranded astronauts*

*Research **sacred geometry** and **cybernetics** (sound)*

Extensive books and information exist about those who have gone beyond the mind's veils through mystical, near-death and out-of-body experiences.

The scientific, spiritual and secular resources available to us are endless.

Better yet, day or night, head into your back yard and discover the gifts, the patterns and systems in nature, that remind us that we are not alone.

The Veiled State

In our veiled state of awareness, Divine Intelligence,
our Soul, is always leading us toward enlightenment.

All experiences are helpful—in joy—toward this end, even if our ego mind
feels differently and is caught in goopy loops of fear, guilt, blame or shame.

The Divine Vibrations/Frequencies of Joy and Peace (Coherent Light)
are what we are made of. Therefore, they are always present. Always!

All we need to do is to ask for Love's Help Within.

When we trust Love, we are working miracles.

Don't worry if your mind doesn't see this.

Miracles are a felt sense of peace.

They do show up in the world,

even if we don't always see

at first with our own eyes.

And, often, we do see.

The world does shift.

The mind's veils

dissolve in

goodwill.

Love Sees Only Beauty

We could look to any number of apparently
unbeautiful scenes within us and in the world.

Yet, within Divine Intelligence, nothing is seen unbeautiful.
We are creators of unspeakable power and, often, grace.
Divine Intelligence sees only what is true, our Radiant Light.

Only mind/ego/fear sees the unseemingly,
seemingly less than perfect and whole.

Never fear fear.
Ego isn't real.

Trust Love to undo what's not true.

Reincarnation and the *Felt Sense*

At around age 29,[53] I began my "official" search for answers regarding my mystical experiences and my questions about God, suffering, why people are cruel to each other and self, and why I couldn't remember where I come from.

Here's a story that occurred near the beginning of this search. I was living in Phoenix, Arizona. My radiant dad, who has always shined, came for a visit. I was working part-time at the A.R.E. Medical Clinic health store. (A.R.E. stands for Association of Research and Enlightenment.) The A.R.E. Medical Clinic was founded by Dr. William McGarey, a physican. Dr. McGarey is a student of Edgar Cayce. Edgar Cayce (d. 1945) is one of the most famous psychics in the world. Over 14,000 word-for-word readings by Cayce are on file. A considerable number, sixty-percent, are health/medical related.

My dad and I were in a restaurant. He asked me, to my unexpected surprise, if I believed in reincarnation. I said I did though I felt it didn't matter to believe in it and did not focus on it in my studies. He said, "What if it's not true?" I knew that having a belief in reincarnation is not necessary to find our Inner Light, yet, the response that came from within me helped to strengthen an expanding awareness within myself regarding the value of trusting my intuition or gnosis. I do not know how my response affected my dad, or if he even remembers the conversation. However, I remember this moment.

This is what I said, "What I live a happier life because I believe in reincarnation? What if I live a miserable life if I don't?" Of course, someone could live a perfectly joyful, peaceful life not believing in reincarnation, or a miserable life believing in it. The valuable information is, "What is the feeling within the belief?" Then comes, "Do I want to keep this belief? Is there something I'd like to shift around it?" As the value of trusting our intuition expands, the willingness to go inward for better information expands. I went inward for information at a young age. I would imagine many go within. Do we even realize what we're doing? Yes, we do! Divine Intelligence always knows what it is doing.

---

53 We are immersed within, affected by and made up of infinite invisible, yet profoundly sensitive fields. This is well documented in science. We are all affecting and are affected by everything within the cosmos.

Children and the *Felt* Sense

Children are astonishing. If we listen to what they are describing (remember, a child's vocabulary and sense of the world is different a grown-ups so it can take gentle, patient listening), it becomes obvious that they are feeling into what they are experiencing. They are processing, responding peacefully or reacting to inner fear.

Does this sound like someone else you know? It is from this feeling place, we inquire. Feel within yourself as you listen to yourself, to children, to other grown-ups. You may be surprised by what you come to recognize. We are wise to listen gently, filled with grace.

We are Divinely Radiant Intelligence.
We are safely held in Coherent Light.

Each of us travels the perfect path to awakening.

Making a mistake to awakening along the way is impossible.
If this seems hard to believe, see yourself or another as a tiny, terrified child who doesn't know what to do or where to turn.

As the veils dissolve in our mind, we awaken to the the Light that we are and that we are immersed within.

When we awaken we really create!

Equine as Calm, Aware Guide

*It is well known that when a horse feels comfortable and relaxed
she will lick her lips in your presence. She may even yawn.
When comfortably grazing or at rest she will lower
her head, flooding endorphins[54] into her brain.*

*Horses are gentle prey animals. They are food for others.
As prey, they are profoundly aware of their surroundings.
A horse's vision is virtually 360° due to the placement of their eyes.
Horses have eyes on the sides of their heads to support soft, wide vision.
You can be sure they are aware of your presence far before you become
aware of theirs, and not just visually. They, quite literally, feel your presence.*

*They are not only aware of physical presence they read our intentions toward
them. They read how we are moving, how we are really feeling (not our
opinion of how we are feeling) and the pictures in our mind. Horse language
is a language of vision, physical movement, subtle vibration and pictures. Any
animal trainer will share to think in pictures what we want an animal to do. Some
know to add to send the feeling of an action. We can learn much from horses
by learning about how to approach them. If we stand tall and aggressively
approach them, straight on, hips and shoulders in a direct line toward their
body, focusing intently on them, they may respond as if we are a predator. This
is how predators approach. Plus, we are bi-pedal—standing tall, eyes locked
on, by nature. We look to a horse as if we're ready to pounce on our prey!*

*To make friends with a horse, speak heart to heart long before you are near. Use your
voice/sound as well. Approach slowly, at a side angle, toward a shoulder, not directly
toward their head. Keep your heart open, your mind still and your voice soft. Breathe
into your heart. Stay alert, in a kind, open space. Keep your vision soft, not focused on
them. This helps heighten your own awareness, vision and sense of their expansive field
(and yours!), and they may relax. You are getting to know a friend. Do not approach a
horse's head until they invite you in. You will sense if you are gaining their trust. If you are
reluctant to approach, a horse sees and feels your reluctance. It may leave the area,
sensing that its presence is distressing for you. A respectful, trust building approach is
to softly observe, perhaps even to squat near the ground a bit away, connecting your
heart with theirs. Horses are curious, smart and gentle by nature. Assuming a non-
threatening posture and giving them space to come to you is enormously honoring.*

---

54 Endorphins are neurotransmitters. They help us feel good, resembling opiates in their abilities to
reduce or dissolve pain and induce a feeling of wellbeing. Ref: Wikipedia

Equine as Calm, Aware Guide
(continued)

Horses do not need to be broken to gain their cooperation. As with a human or other another animal, "breaking a horse" breaks its spirit. Ask your heart if this is how you want to be treated? As we spend time honoring a horse, they respect us and will do almost anything for us, as we often do when we are treated as valuable. (There is a powerful method for making friends with a horse you want to ride called Join-Up.) Horses have fought human wars, plowed our fields and kept us fed and warm. They have taken us places farther than we could ever go ourselves, physically and spiritually. Horses are now being used to help calm the nervous systems of humans, especially those with highly sensitive (high functioning) nervous systems, often called autism. Animals have long been recognized for their healing powers because they are so deeply aware.

It is wise to respect and get to know animals. They will share their secrets.

What helps you feel safe and comfortable in any environment?

Look to the relations in your life. Be aware of where you place value.

Trust that slowness, observation and gentle care hold exquisite gifts.

Ponder how your actions reflect a sense of whether you feel safe.

Explore what it means to hold safe, honoring space for others.

*Gentle observation and respectful interaction
reveals more than we can possibly imagine.*

We all deserve to be treated in this way.

When we are not treated kindly,

look for the Light within.

We are astonishing!

What About Unkindness and Cruelty

The world is packed with stories of horror.

View such the stories with Love's awareness.

Forgive all perpetrators with Love's Divine Light.

*Our greatest stories of pain often reveal our Divine gifts
and launch us swiftly on the path toward the Inner Light.*

Bring to heart stories in your world that revealed great insight?

Look directly at relations that you tie your value, your worth, to.

Your worth is set. You are Divine Radiance. You are eternal Light.

This is always true. When we leave form, we see with real sight.

The adventure for all is to remember this is true for everyone.

If another seems to cause you distress, trust the gift is true.

Go within YOU.

For inspiration regarding awakening adventures...

Rent the beautiful film "Journey into Dyslexia"

Open a Golden Gateway

Holding a heartfelt intention opens an inner gateway.

*Our focus on vibrationally felt Lovingkindness and goodwill
is powerful beyond measure for expanding our perception.*

*Imagine a Sun Bow spiral, a Golden spiral, or a White spiral.
(We are immersed in sun bow light. It's just that most only
see such colors when atmospheric conditions are ideal.)*

*Adventure with Radiant Light visualizations for your meditations
Your inner experience may grow more beautiful and deeper.*

Hold a deeply honoring space for what occurs within.

Consider journaling or drawing your poignant insights.

Share with Divine Intelligence that you are interested.

*You are a gift to this world.
Your presence is exquisite.
We all need what you are.*

Please share your Light.

Adventuring with "Going Home"

*So many of us know consciously that this world, where so many suffer,
is not a real place even though this seems inconceivable to our mind.*

*In the year 2001, at 97, my grandmother passed over. She called me from Heaven.
Gram, as we called her, lived in her later years in Michigan, near family. I was living
in Bellingham, Washington at the time. Before I moved to Bellingham I had a feeling
she may not last much longer. Sure enough she passed within a month after my
move. Her passing came shortly after 9/11. I was deeply resonating with my new
home, and, given my belief (or non-belief rather) in actual death, I considered
not returning for fear that if further attacks came I wouldn't be able to return to
Bellingham and my dog. Note my fear. I also felt that Gram was with me more now
than ever. Yet, in my heart, I could not not go to her funeral and be with my family.
And, of course, I was able to make my way safely back to Bellingham. Soon after I
returned, I had a dream. Gram called me on the phone to tell me she was fine. We
spoke for sometime. I don't remember much of the content of the conversation.
What I do remember is that I was curious about her whereabouts. When I asked her
a science question, she said in her wondrously Light giggly voice, "I don't know Laur!
I'll go get my mother!" That woke me up! I soon remembered a dear friend's story
about her father's passing. Her father had been a chemist and a doctor. After he
died she spoke with him in the dream state. She asked where he was. His answer
was "Quad C4." She didn't know where that was. I have remembered this story for
years and years. Just recently, while watching the film Apollo 13 for the umteenth
time, I kept hearing the astronauts say, "Quad C!" I had never caught this before. I
promptly did an internet search and discovered Quad C is related to audio (sound)
systems. This makes perfect sense. The movement aspect of the Infinite is sound,
wind, color, motion, etc., what scientists call the physics of quality. Such physics are
subtle and gross frequency. All frequency rests within the Ultimate Container, Divine
stillness. I contacted my friend immediately to ask her sense of this discovery. She felt
it was accurate. Her father was telling her he was vibration, frequency and sound.
Her father was an astounding mathematician—being trained as a chemist—yet he
knew she wasn't! He offered her a language she would understand, with a delightful
twist that sent us on a quest of wonder into the meaning of Quad C4. He must
be giggling like crazy. I can feel the flutter. These are only two stories compared
to the literature that exists on communications with those beyond the veil.*

What an adventure! We are beyond stellar!

*Do you have a story to share about not
dying and how it helped to comfort?*

The Glorious Grey

Gandolf the Grey? Nope.

A grey world? A grey mind? Yep!

We know all about black and white.

We're just not sure what to do about the grey.

Let it be okay.

Adventure with the grey.

Garnish the grey with your radiance.

Light up the grey with your Light.

This morning we were heading for an early morning family chiropractic adjustment—the family that cracks together, cracks up better together. We decided to visit a drive through coffee bar for the long suburban commute to an astonishingly radiant Chicagoland-based practitioner. I was riding shotgun. (I'll let that phrase pass.) My gaze was free to roam. I noticed the grey snow. The grey sky. The grey road. The grey rock. The grey bold. That is, the bold and radiant folks journeying to all sorts of places, in all sorts of ways. We know what to do with the black and the white. What do we do with the grey? We look inside our heart, in this holy, radiantly now moment. We remember we dream. It is our choice to dream happy dreams or unhappy dreams. We are to relish them all. This wakes us up. For today, do not be hard on yourself if you're feeling an unhappy dream. Share your feelings with the Light Within. Share your worries with the angels. Ask to be guided by your radiance, your deeply-feeling Light. Feel your pain. Let it be okay for all. Hold a hand. Yours will feel held just the same. You are warm.

Trust your Light.

(A word on the grey. In Truth, there are only two states, Love or fear. Only Love is real. There is no real grey. There is only the extension of Life and Light. Grey is an illusion.[55])

---

55 There is only Love and Light. It may be important to note that some beings understand this Truth, others not so much. Look to guides who teach of the Light. Mostly look within your own heart for this

Inner Storm Chasers

Children, and we grown-ups, can be great Loves and great whiners.
Whine-mind is always an inner storm chaser. Loving a good twister!

We do not serve to respond to a child's or a grown-up's whine.
Gentleness is encouraged to help him/her (or us) to smoothly shift.

Both Love and fear/shame are present inside us all. As we assist a child to use
a kind, normal tone of voice in making a request he/she is enabled to find Love.
If a child is wary or triggered in any way, Inner Light awareness is harder to find.

If the inner child is immersed in unkind whine mind, be gently aware.
I will ask a little one, "How do you feel inside when you are speaking?"

Helping us to become aware of our inner state is invaluable for all.
Otherwise, a being may entrain to trusting that treating others in
a disrespectful way is helpful and okay for trying to meet a need.
Look to a world of abuse, war, murder and suicide if we wonder.

It is vital to check in with ourselves to make sure WE are listening.
(If it's not a good time for listening, let the other know in a kind way.)

Children and grown-ups perceive in multi-dimensions and often
without words, or with limited vocabulary. We may not seem to
make sense to each other when hearts are actually deeply aware
and trying to share something that seems important to us.

Those who are trying to communicate have something to share.

At any age we are communicating with each other 24/7.
We are communicating always regarding whether we are
listening to Love/One awareness or to our ego/fear mind.
Both states of mind feel very real to us so slowing helps us
listen within to ensure we are tuned to the Light channel.

---

knowledge. There is nothing to fear in either case. All will eventually awaken to our Still Radiant Eternal Nature.

Precious Gratitude

We are infinitely more precious than we imagine.
Relax into the Light of peace, gratitude and joy.
We are dancing a perfectly choreographed
curriculum to awaken from the dreamtime.

What fear-mind believes are "problems,"
are exquisitely powerful, alchemically
healing moments to trust Perfect Love.

We never really left Home.
We just dimmed our Divine
Perception Mechanisms.

We forgot we are One.

Life at work, at home, in community and at play
is an extreme adventure into remembering we
never really left the Home of Absolute Being.

The Pulse of Life

When you wake up tomorrow, lay in bed for a moment.

Keep your eyes closed. Take in what comes.

Sounds. Sensations. Feelings. Tension. Release.

Embrace the sensory without attaching to story.

Invite the Light of You to become present.

What does your body feel like?

Can you feel the plasma of air?

What does your environment sound like?

Eventually draw yourself to a comfortable sitting position.

Gently allow Light to flood into your awareness.

Light is your natural state so no effort is needed.

Notice the pulse of life within and around you.

The World is a Dream

*If our Teachers of Peace are to be trusted,
pain and suffering is a truly unnatural state.*

*Thanks to the efforts of millions of our hearts,
our dreaming is written in all human traditions.*

*Our awakening is written in the art of the cosmos.
Our awakening is written in the Light of One Heart.*

*This may feel hard to digest given the attachments and the suffering
we have here in this world. Yet, pain is the evidence for pain's unreality.*

Can this be proved? That LOVE IS?

*Love the world with all your might.
Affirm Life's grace and joy and peace.*

Do this for your whole radiant Life.

And, you will see for yourself.

*We are the dreamer. Divine Intelligence is here.
Masters know this. Fear needs our Love to wake up.*

As we trust gentle, loving kindness, we speed our awakening.

And we are able to have some pretty stunning adventures on the way.

Make Everything an Adventure

Relish the distasteful. Swim in the unglorious adventure.
Giggle brushing your teeth. Try brushing someone else's.
If you walk into a restroom that is occupied, laugh.
If you have green stuff in your teeth, belly laugh!
If someone is upset, go inside your heart.
Ask what your heart can fully extend.
Savor the experience of Life's fare.

There is a splendid scene in the film *Star Trek Generations*. The character Data, an android, has received an emotion chip. Data has always wanted to feel to human emotions. In this scene, he is with friends in 10 Forward, the ship's lounge. Gynen, the bartender, serves Data and Geordi a new beverage she's just received into the bar. Data takes a sip of the drink and makes a strange face and noise. Because he has never experienced emotion he's not sure how to describe his experience. Yet, from Data's expression, his friends can tell the drink is not pleasing to him. Gynen says, "You hate it?" And, he says, "Yes, I hate this!" Then, he takes another glass, quickly drinking it down, exclaiming, "I hate this! This is revolting!" Then he grabs another. Data is enjoying the adventure of experiencing human emotion. His enthusiasm overpowers his distaste.

There is no Truth that says, "Life is a drag. Let's make it worse."

Make all your activities and emotions adventures, including distaste!

Here's another example of taste: I've spent a lot of time in the wilderness, some of it climbing mountains. I love it. I love going up and up and up and up! When climbing it is necessary to carry fairly heavy packs laden with ropes and metal gear for technical (dangerous/exposed) routes, plus a tent and sleeping bag, food, clothes, water and other supplies. This sort of journey is not the idea of a good time for many folks, but our love of mountains makes every aspect sheer pleasure, including intense sensations.

What in your life do you enjoy so much that you know only joy and are willing to endure, and perhaps relish, the adventure of the intensity of doing it?

Now, explore a memory in a sadness or madness adventuring moment. Allow whatever comes up as perfect. Allow the sensations to dissolve.

Balto

Balto is a canine hero.

A fearless dog of selfless giving.

Selfless giving reminds us what we are.

We are Divine Radiance. We are safely held.

On February 2, 1925, during a blizzard, Balto courageously
helped to save a town in Alaska from a diphtheria plague.

He was the brave four-legged leader of a dog-sled team.
The team's human driver was Gunnar. A kind, smart man.

Balto led his team for 20 hours and 53 miles bringing medicine.
Their journey was intended to last half that distance.
When the relief team wasn't on hand Balto's team chose
to go on through the blizzard. Strikingly, they arrived
in one-third the time expected by the town of Nome!

(I cried when I read this story.)

A statue of Balto stands in New York City celebrating this feat.

Stories such as these are profoundly helpful to share.
They remind us what we are really doing here. Loving.
Every day you are kind and helpful. Love you for this.

Thank you for all you do to help other people feel worth it.

A key enlightenment teaching is that giving and receiving are identical.[56]
As we give without thought for gain, Life's aware flow naturally expands.

---

56 This is universal law. Bring to mind "karma" or *cause* and *effect*. Only our unkind, critical or ungenerous *deeply felt* thoughts and fears of sharing and equal exchange keep the veils in our mind intact and wonder veiled from our awareness. When we aren't Light generous, we simply don't see/ remember Truth.

Your Light Never Changes

You are Light, true and bright.

Your Divine Radiance never changes. Nope.
How much you are cherished never changes.

The Mix Up makes the case of this you can be sure.
This is the message the wakeful share in all times.

Our heart knows our Unchanging Light and
the Divine Intelligence that animates All Life.

Evidence is everywhere. We are evidence.

Whatever brought you here,
thank you for your Light.

The Author Questions

No one at all suffers beyond our mind's veil. No one.
We are immersed in radiance not wholly perceived.

Can you feel the oscillating glow? I can too.

This world is a miracle, even with all its horrors. So what
lies beyond? Well, it only gets better. Unspeakably better.

My inner life has been active since a young age. A mystical experience,
that I didn't know was mystical, or that there was even such a word as
mystical, was part of my every day experience when I was very young.
(Mystical/metaphysical simply means beyond the physical,
or able to go within and access higher states of awareness
and, in my case, being acutely sensitive to frequency.)

My sensitivity is a felt sense. I am able to feel, and sometimes
see, the mechanics of the dreamtime. I also have cosmic
dreams and insights. For example, as a young child
I knew the speed of light (as humans think of it) was slow. This is accurate.

I somehow knew as a child that the way to return to peace was by
going within. It would be years before I would realize the value of my
natural tendency toward this response, and what a gift it has been.

A few circumstances early in life contrived to ensure that I would be propelled
inward. I would also learn how to trust my felt sense. An unspeakably powerful
event was the physical death of my baby brother. (It would take awhile for me
to get that there is no such thing as real death.) I was five years old. Michael was
born with a heart defect. The surgery to correct the condition was successful. He
lived peacefully among us for three months. Doctors told my parents that it was
best for Michael to remain quiet while his body was healing. He did. Profoundly.
My recollection is that he barely made a peep. That is, until one day. While the
surgery to repair the hole in his heart was successful, what was not successful was
his ability to ward off infection after surgery. At the time, the procedure Michael

underwent to repair his heart involved removing the entire spleen, a key organ in the body's ability to remain in balance. When he got sick, his infant voice sounded for hours. You know this infant scream. It is the scream that all in the vicinity try with the might of the angels to comfort. The doctor kept saying to calm him. We couldn't. After many hours he was taken to the hospital where he died of blood poisoning. My next memory is my mother asking me what outfit to bury him in.

The Author Questions
(continued)

My baby brother was gone. I was shattered.

Michael's departure rocked my world.
I was afraid of losing what was left,
my parents and my older brother.

This experience would help thrust me into questioning everything.
I finally came to know that only Love is real. And death isn't.
This world is transcended by Loving with a Mighty Heart.

What stories in your life feel (or felt) difficult to downright horrific?
How do they assist you to seek within for better information?
Only the mind is veiled. Our Divine Radiance never is.

As we Love and forgive all difficult adventures,
the cosmos is shifting before our very eyes.

Thank you for your deep willingness!
You are the Star of the Universe!

Shine On!

Enlightenment

If you are feeling unloving or unpeaceful it is wise to not suppress these feelings, however, do not act upon them either. Give them to the Inner Light, to God. They are frequencies that will pass through you and dissolve because they are actually not real. Sounds pretty incredible, huh? It's true. Hug your feelings, and let them dissolve. The more we resist our discomfort the more confused we become. Here is why.

What we are feeling is the residue of the original separation trauma in our mind. We must remember and re-remember is that time is an illusion. This is a fact. The separation/veiling/bang event took place only an instant ago!

Astonishing, eh?

All events are actually taking place at once. Wild these facts!
This separation trauma is deeply disturbing to our psyche.
The terror within us is far more intense than we realize.
As we allow all unpeaceful states, fear, anger,
depression, grief, frustration, on and on,
to pass through unresisted they
dissolve. This cannot be
stated too often.
Trust peace.
Within.

Fear is unremembered Love. See all experiences as an adventure. Ask with your heart's might for Love to assist you to trust peace. Love always responds. This is felt-prayer. Indeed, words are meaningless if not deeply felt. As we relax our attachment to judging distress, honoring and allowing feelings to be okay, great healing is occurring. This is the process we call enlightenment. Our mind may object and want us to travel to an even deeper upset state. Think of the image of traveling on a spiral, up or down. This fear is nothing to fear. Fearing the energy-in-motion occurring within us actually veils Love.

A Course in Miracles

*A Course in Miracles is fast becoming one of the
most read and studied documents on the planet.*

*The story of how it came to be is fascinating to explore.
Its scribes were deeply attached to ego's critical mind.*

*The purpose of A Course in Miracles is a course to be studied and practiced.
Love is helping us recognize how relentless and brutal our fear-mind is and how
deeply convinced our mind is that this world is reality, rather than a substitute
illusion veiling Heaven. A Course in Miracles is, perhaps, the most redundant
document on the planet. It clarifies how beautiful and cherished we are and
why we are so messed up. It re-emphasizes in a gazillion ways the fast path
for enlightenment: The Golden Rule of Seeing All Beings as Perfect and Divine
and overlooking all our dreaming errors. The Course is written in such a way—
largely in iambic pentameter—to help flip the switch (think of a circuit breaker
or a router) in our mind from focusing on fear, guilt, shame, blame, the dark
(illusion) to focusing on Light, the only reality. For students, it becomes obvious
that the message is simply to trust the strength of kind and gentle Love.*

*Legions from beyond the veils in our mind are sharing with us to trust Love's kindness.
We sense this Love in our waving particles because our particles
are Divinely Intelligent. We feel Love as peace. Notice how awake
beings do not attack. Think of individuals you respect, Buddha, Jesus,
Mother Theresa, Gandhi, Martin Luther King, Jr., Brahma.*

Look to models of Love when you are feeling the separation in your mind.

*There is no judgment in being fearful. Love knows we are often afraid
to trust Love. We simply allow our awareness to return to peace
when it feels ready to do so. This ensures that we do not store fear
that keeps our awareness veiled to Love's Divine Intelligence.*

Ego (Fear) Drama

Spiritual teachings (and our heart!) remind us of our beauty and wholeness and how cherished we are. They also help us to see how brutal our ego-mind (fear) is.

We are never upset for the reason we think, say the Illuminated Beings.
We are upset because we have forgotten who, what and where we are!

Think of ego as all about "mine" and "me" forgetting the Light of Being.

When something feels upsetting, the deluge from the "mine of me" is astonishing. Ego is tricky. Unconditional Love never admonishes. Ego can be timid or forceful, and it fears harsh judgment and change. When I find myself spinning, I go within.

Fear-filled thoughts are chaotic and weak because they are illusions ("me" created). Yet, because we have the Source-power/Love to create our own reality, when we trust fear, when we give fear our Source-power, our Light, so fear expands. It seems very real. And we create a reality that seems fearful. This is collective science. Gently allow fearful thoughts to float away. They will dissolve, and we will have more passion for doing what we love. It is wise to be gentle with self and to focus on what feels important right now.

Divine Intelligence uses everything to help us remember the Light.

If you are willing, bring into your awareness an emotional upset.

Love yourself for being willing to go through this adventure.

As you hold this circumstance in your heart,
share within your heart that you are safe.
Give your feelings to Love. Honor you.

Rest peacefully with this awareness.

Adventuring with Self-Honesty

Extreme adventures require adventurous self-honesty.
You are brave and up to this wildly truthful journey.

Have you ever done something you love doing with someone with whom
you don't resonate? And, you found you were not having all that much fun?
Now, bring to awareness doing this same activity with someone you adore.
(Do not judge such experiences or individuals. Just be aware of sensation.)

Hold the awareness, the felt sense within you, of these experiences.

For the purpose of unveiling our mind and becoming more aware of our
own radiance and the astonishing wonder that we are immersed within,
next time this happens, be aware not so much of who you are with
or what you are doing, but rather with what you are trusting.

Are you trusting Unconditional Love or ego?
Again, no guilt. Just honest inquiry.

(Remember, ego is merely the belief in our mind that we are not safe and
that we are separate from stuff or people we don't seem to like all that well.)

Awakening from our veiled state is a real adventure.
It is by far the most extreme adventure possible.

As we realize that only our own mind is veiled to the Great Rays of Golden and
Sun Bow Light that extend outwardly and inwardly in infinite directions from
our core, we become more interested in what we are trusting right now.

We see our experiences in a new Light! Our darker moments are gifts!
Perhaps make some Great Ray Awareness notes,
and remember to Love yourself deeply in
moments you find yourself in fear.

You are astonishing Light!

Trust Your Divine Intelligence

You are Divine Intelligence.

You are Love.

We needn't look far to find this information everywhere in spiritual and native traditions and in science. So what's up?

Our critical mind is veiling astonishing wonder.

We are blocking our Divine Intelligence.

To wake up, Enlightened Ones say,

"Become like an empty cup."[57]

When our mind is full, we block what is true.

Self-trust and empty, non-critical mind is vital.

We must trust Self enough to go within to Love.

As we release our mind's criticisms, we are clearer receivers for Divine Intelligence.

Self-trust is not arrogant. It is gentle awareness.

Ego is arrogantly looking for affirmation of value.

Our mini-me van is vulnerable to Radiant Light. We might be unspeakably amazed at the sight!

Self-trusting awareness flows when we are at peace. Self-trusting awareness knows to disregard fears and worries. Trust the value of your life here, and your life beyond here.

---

57 A key teaching of Jesus and Buddha. Remember, we are already awake. We are already enlightened/aware that we are Light. We need only wake up from a dream of not peace.

The Science of Resonance

We, our awareness and our bodies, are subtle oscillating magnetic resonators.
Our physical form is an electro-magnet, a Light crystalline magnet.
Our awareness sends, receives and expands Love and fear signals.
Everything in existence is oscillating and resonating. Sometimes, this is
happening too fast for the eye to detect.[58] Yet, we feel these oscillations.
And, truly, the forms we see every day are moving in this way!

Have you ever felt uncomfortable in a situation? Have you ever felt at peace in a
situation? Have you ever felt a pit in your stomach? A pain in your heart or in your
head? A lump in your throat? Have you ever felt your voice vibrating? This is your
awareness tuning to and affecting our collectively coherent Inner Light or our
collectively felt ego/fear/dissonance (disrupted coherent light/energy blocks).

You are "manigesting"[59] in this very moment.

Our visual system is oscillating and holographic.
It is a projector for viewing a cosmic hologram.

Everything about us is resonating and holographic.
Our world is so dense feeling most of
us don't spend lots of time contemplating such things. Yet, we
are pendulums moving fast, infinitely fast,[60] between action and
rest. We don't realize this is occurring—unless we are accessing
higher states. Bodies are slow oscillators compared to Light.

Ponder the following. All Life resonates. Life resonates with coherent
oscillations. Coherency is pure awareness. Here in our amnesic
dreamtime state where we cannot fully remember our origin, unless we
are deeply attuned to Love's Radiance/Divine Intelligence, we tend
to trust fear/dissonance and systems that support dissonance.

---

58   Itzak Bentov's *Stalking the Wild Pendulum: On the Mechanics of Conscious* covers this subject in stunning detail that is easy for non-scientists to grasp. He is hilarious and his diagrams are de-Light-fully clear.
59   Manifesting and digesting and gestating – a new word!
60   Infinite speed is the same as stillness. Refer to Bentov and other scientific research.

Yet all fear is merely disrupted frequency. This is mind/ego.

As we place focus on Light, on peace, our awareness returns to coherency. Next time you are in a group notice what seems peaceful and what doesn't. Be sure not to judge the circumstance. Simply be aware. You are a pendulum.

You can strengthen your coherent resonance anytime you ask within.

The Science of Resonance
(continued)

We resonate with…gravitate toward…the strongest frequency in a given situation until it dawns on us that only we can choose Truth/Light from within.

When we shift into peace, we help smooth everyone's oscillations.

We might even fly if we didn't think so much!

Here is a coherency restoring technique:

Focus softly and gently on your breath.

Smile and exhale. Smiling releases endorphins.

Tap your fingertips in a radiant beat over your heart.

Light a candle and put on some soothing music.
Bring to mind something that cracks you up.
Play and joy activates our heart's magnet.
Slowly move in flowing postures focusing
on your breathing and feeling your body.
Spend time doing something peaceful that
causes you to forget about the world entirely.

There is a Light song playing in your heart.

Do you feel lit?

Human Babies

Babies are on a mission of Light, yet, like us, they may not know it.

All beings born into our world have a veiled mind. We cannot remember fully where we come from and what is to happen next. All arrive with free will and the essence of a trajectory that holds the potential to help us "enlighten." By trusting peace we gently remove our focus from the fear matrix in our own mind. Unconditional loving works.

Our life is our curriculum for awakening, if we so choose.

Babes are born with their own programming (think of DNA, personality and more). We arrive with a sense of indivi"dual"ity. Alone and unified. We have a dual purpose.

In Truth, we are One, an undivided Absolute Being.

Ego/fear-mind is easy to observe in children. It is a lack of peace over anything. A sense that says, "I might not be safe. Someone might be forgetting about me." Fear in the mind feels like, upset, or Love unremembered. We believe in feelings.

There is also within us all the knowledge of the reality of what we are, which is Divine Intelligence. As such, we possess the capabilities of Divine Intelligence.

We have within us an exquisite peace and a knowledge that is always present. We have an innate sense of our unity, our gifts and our ability to complete our mission—whatever that looks like for each of us. Our mission is only revealed on a need to know basis. If we were told what is to come next, we might miss important steps.[61]

As we assist children to feel Light, we feel our own.

Cherish babies. They are Divine wonders!

---

61   Information in *A Course in Miracles*, obtained within. Information that is accurate is accessible to us all.

Trusting Peace Helps Everyone

While it may feel disorienting to us, the massive increase in the number of humans presenting with highly sensitive nervous systems is evidence of our awakening. Highly sensitive beings are less veiled to Divine Intelligence however such beings are also highly sensitive to disruptive/dissonant energetics coming from within the collective.

Additionally, like us, they do not have their full awareness, their full memory of Divine Intelligence.

We can explain this circumstance to at least some.

We need to calm and hold a safe, honoring Light space for everyone to go gently within.

Dissonant energy is not real, but it feels profoundly real to us, and, especially, to those with highly expanded nervous systems. Think of the pebble in the pond analogy. Imagine tossing a pebble into the middle of a glassy pond. This action creates coherent, concentric circles. Now, imagine doing a belly flop into the middle of the pond and watch what happens to the circles. The splash is like our mind-energy, our thoughts, feelings and actions of upset coming from the collective and especially from those we resonate with. Disruptive frequencies within the mind block awareness of the peace and Divine Intelligence that is always present within. Those with expanded nervous systems are far more sensitive to all states, the Real One and the false.

When WE are calm and peaceful others are naturally assisted to attune to peace. Love/Coherent Light is fail-safe, i.e., this cannot be faked. Peace is always present but it cannot be felt by faking peace or joy. As we face the fear inside, it dissolves naturally.

As we rest our busy, churning minds and attune our heart's crystalline magnet to the frequencies and harmonics of Divine Intelligence/Coherent Light that surround and permeate existence, we support each other to regain a sense of inner peace.

As we enter the high sensitive's world and adventure with them, rather expecting them to move into our mind/world, which, for them, feels energetically chaotic/incoherent, we serve a collective healing for us all. Even if such beings do not respond peacefully, we find ourselves being more at peace within ourselves and better able to assist.

Miracles of internal and external communication become possible.

Oscillating Explorations

There is a simple way to grasp how every one of us assists the mind to wake up. Read the following, then close your eyes, draw a few gentle, calming breaths, and activate your heart's magnet. Without effort, visualize yourself, not as a physical body, but as oscillating waves of radiant Coherent Light, a moving sun bow of frequency, sound, color and wind, within and as the cosmos. Allow yourself a few moments to drop the body and feel your wave-particles gently oscillating. Gently release your thinking mind.

Suspend your disbelief in your Inner Light.

Effortlessly allow this experience to come forth into your awareness. Your breathing may deepen or become almost still. Trust what occurs when you do this exercise, knowing with all your heart that you are safely held in the Inner Light of all Life.

From a young age, something within me knew that my felt sense of energy was very helpful information.

My trust in my own felt sense eventually helped me to integrate what may be being felt by those with highly expanded, high functioning nervous systems.

Children born these days are coming in with far less mind veiling. These beings have been called Indigo Children, Crystal Children, Rainbow Children and on and on. The colors refer to colors in the auras of these children. We all have colors in our aura.

We are being asked to release our self-judgments and judgments about others to help us remember what and where we really are. It is important to be non-reactive to upsets. We are asking ourselves through our Inner Light because we are so asleep here.

Our heart knows that no one of us is more extraordinary than another.

We are all extraordinary, and we are all Enlightened Masters!

Beliefs are Astonishingly Powerful

*Our greatest spiritual teachers have asserted the power of belief for eons.
Science has long confirmed the universal law of resonant attraction.
Our deeply felt thoughts are quantumly powerful creators.*

*It does not take much effort to look around ourselves and
recognize that we are where we are because we believed
some things and we did not believe some other things.*

*In sacred geometry studies I learned that if we don't give our focus to ego
thoughts, the frequencies of such thoughts will dissolve/be cleansed at
the end of a day or at the dawn of a new day. This is why the
ancients cherished the shifting times, dusk and dawn.
Eclipse times are also Divinely intensely
healing times. Frequencies of
the Divine are being
secured within our
cosmic mind.
Love's lines
to One.*

Geometries of Culture

Many years ago, I had a wild dream. I was standing outside in an enormous field looking into the sky. The sky functioned as an immense three-dimensional television screen. Onto this sky-screen colossal shapes were being projected, one by one. I remember a cube and several other shapes. Each gigantic shape rotated slowly, high in the sky, while the voice of a male narrator explained the shape's significance. (Imagine a narrator from a Discovery or National Geographic channel program.) The narrator described each shape in extraordinary detail, including the qualities and mathematics of the forms. I do not have a mind for grasping such detail, and certainly not without the Big Picture. I was trying with all my might to grasp what this narrator was sharing with me. What I remember clearly is the last shape and what the narrator shared about all the shapes. The final shape was very intricate. There were lots of clear diamonds in this form. (I would learn later on that the diamond shape is how higher dimensional form is represented in our 4D world). Running through the middle of this exquisitely intricate form was a clear elongated diamond illuminated more brightly that the other sections, so it shone more overtly within the overall form. Then, I noticed, at the very base of the illumined diamond, another form, a human figure! No features, just the shape of a human. I became excited, for this felt like some place I could go.

The narrator shared that all cultures are based on geometries. This felt so right and so remarkable. Could this be accurate I wondered? Of course it was! I woke up with amazing recall. A curious piece for me was that I'd been on a deeply spiritual/mystical path my whole life, and, with at least ten or twelve years of research (at the time this dream occurred) to help explain and corroborate my own mystical experiences and inner knowing. While I've had dreams with other worldly seeming technologies, I did not recall ever encountering or considering geometry or mathematics in my spiritual research, though I understood science as deeply significant to our learning. Holy multi-dimensional awareness blower! I knew I had to find out what had just happened! I headed for the internet. I'm not sure what phrase I typed in Google™, but rather quickly I stumbled upon the site of Dr. Robert Gilbert of Vesica.org. Dr. Gilbert had recently created some DVDs about sacred geometry that could be ordered. I was on the phone near that day. When they arrived, I stuck like glue to the couch and television screen. I watched the DVDs over and over. They were packed with wonder. Better yet, Dr. Gilbert talked science that made sense to me. I was stunned. My college science classes always sent me spiraling because I knew I could get this stuff, but how it was taught was freaky for how I am wired. It was like all the connective tissue had been sucked out of the material. (This is no criticism to teachers or to textbook creators. I am wired by subtle Light.) Dr. Gilbert is an especially noteworthy and brilliant instructor. He is a former U.S. Marine Corps Instructor in Nuclear-Biological-Chemical Warfare Survival. Since leaving the service in 1985, he has conducted independent research into the geometric basis of modern science and new technologies.[62] He has studied the traditions of many ancient cultures, and, due to his analytical mind and his training in biological systems, he has been able to assimilate data from all sorts of sources to help us generate a broader view of the mechanics of the Divine Intelligence operating within our world (our dream hologram[63]). Moreover, Dr. Gilbert's ability to articulate the information in language that is accessible is astounding. I highly recommend his work.

Perhaps this is the moment to address that there is no such thing as real "evil," as in something being equally powerful (or different than) Love. This concept is quite new in the realm of humanity.[64] This is a dream concept. A deeply felt belief in such a concept makes the absence of Love in all sorts of manifestations as (such as unloving beings and unloving circumstances) appear real to those who believe in such things. (Enlightened beings are capable of knowing only the Light, which is all that is real.) Temporary manifestations of what seem like the opposite of Love are a wild dream idea.

Our deeply felt thoughts are creative. Unkind forms may appear if we believe deeply in their existence. Our infinitely powerful mind may cause them to come into being. Yet, like our own forms, they are not real in the sense that they are not eternal. They are simply our own fear made temporarily manifest. For example, bring to mind when we are unkind to someone. The chances that they will be kind to us are compromised. We may seem like a demon/evil, which is a recently invented concept. All "evil" is simply a temporary amnesia of Love/a lack of Love/Love unrecognized. The cure is forgiveness of self and other. We are One Mind actually, but, from our perspective, it seems like we are "more than One" so this is why we are taught to forgive all of our false perceptions.

---

62 Reference information obtained from Dr. Gilbert's Vesica.org biography.

63 It is vital to keep in mind that everything we experience comes from mind and awareness, not our bodies. Because our mind is deeply veiled to our natural state as Pure Awareness, which always recognizes its fundamental unity with all life, our mind-created world is often, accurately, called a dreamtime. Paradise is all around, we simply do not fully perceive it yet.

64 Research the origin of "evil" or "devil." Jesus is quite clear that evil/shadow is not real. It is in our mind.

Practice inner leadership. Listen gently within and to those around you. Listen for the call for Love and the response of Love. Let go of thoughts, especially thoughts that distract and keep the mind focused on loopy hoops of assumption and judgment drawing you out of this instant into concerns for future or distress from what is past.

It takes exceptional focus to remember Love, especially when one or more join in the forgetfulness of our radiance. Bring to mind antennas. We are antennas. Held apart our antenna's Inner Light signal receiving capacity is weaker than if joined. Brought together a signal is strengthened. When we are collectively focusing on Truth, we are waking up. When we are collectively focusing on stories that manifest illusions of separation, such illusions manifest. This is why it is vital to journey within during upset.

The cool thing is that mis-creations are limited to this world. Whether they are the horrors that fill our world, or horrors that we seem to experience in what feels to be an altered state, these manifestations are contained only within this world. They do not extend into reality, into the heaven, the paradise, we never really left. As we allow the fear within, that we believe is causing our upsets to be okay, and as we share these upsets with Divine Intelligence, they dissolve. This increases the Light quotient within everyone's awareness.

We offer a great service each time we trust Love rather than fear.

Offer Comfort

Offer comfort. Only Light is real.

Love is always the answer.

Love has no opposite.

Love is fail-safe.

Offering comfort may seem offensive to down right wrong to our ego.

Simply ask deep in your heart, "How can I help us remember Love?"

The Raw and Radiant Truth[65]

Our human mind's understanding of Life is deeply limited.
Our heart's understanding of Life is deeply felt and known.

We are immersed within Life at all times. There is nothing that is not alive.

As best you can, take care of your mind
and your physical body as temples of Life.

Do not feel guilty for perceived errors or a body
or a mind that sometimes seems to be broken.

We deserve to be well nourished and well hydrated. In a balanced state,
it is easier to maintain a radiant connection with our own Divine Intelligence.
We can have a vibrant, healthy physical form and forget entirely about Love.
We can have a disfigurement or a unique quality and remember Love fully.

It is most important to trust only kind thoughts and to never judge.
If we hold to unkind thoughts and actions that do not feel Loving,
the inner storm chases away the healing benefits of healthy foods.

Adventure with feeding humanity's kids foods that enliven body and soul.
If we consume denatured foods, it is much harder to maintain balance.
Forgive those who enjoy profit from denaturing food. Strive to learn more.
If we honor our bodies and the food we place within it, we see the results.
If we do not care about how we treat all our bodies, we see the results.

Plant a family garden using organic materials and seeds or seedlings.
Fall in love with the process of caretaking that which takes care of us.

---

65 *The Raw Truth* is also the title of an interesting book on raw nutrients by Jordan Rubin.

Shapes of Perception

When I straighten my hair I look a few years younger.
The shift is palpable to me and on the faces of friends.

Shape is a whole lot of perception.

How often do we accept and dismiss on the basis of shape?

A heavy person. A thin person.

A boy or a girl quite round or quite tall.

Thoughts and feelings have shape.
Thoughts and feeling have form.

It's not what we do. It is how we feel about what we do.
Is our Oneness felt, or is a sense of separation magnified?

When we enter our Still Core the thoughts that come
are shaped Lightly. They are well formed and helpful.

Thousands of years of painful learning can
be saved by entering our Still Radiant Core.

Form and Sound are Data Carriers

Shape, sound, vibration, color, scent, everything is packed with Divine Intelligence.

Form and sound is packed with data. This is common knowledge to scientists. For a theatrical reminder, remember the film Contact with Jodi Foster? The radio signal received from space is packed with massive amounts of data. While the film was fictional, the information about sound containing vast amounts of data is accurate.

Dr. Robert Gilbert, a scientist, teacher and geometer, shares poignantly in his lectures regarding the massive data contained in form. He describes and shows how, when some proteins are misshapen within the body, horrible disease can manifest. And, we know that viruses are difficult to destroy. Why? Their shape is hard to penetrate.

Enlightened Masters sometimes present images of geometric forms to their students. Forms are data packets. Think of a quartz crystal computer chip with data. Students tune into Divinely Intelligent information merely by gazing upon an image. Add sound and other elements to sort of experience and awareness can be expanded. Yet, information cannot be accessed/unpacked without appropriate consciousness.

*As one student learns, we all learn (awaken actually).
Recall, we are One Mind, a Singularity of Awareness.*

As determined by our readiness, when we are Loving, data is simply available to us. All data is already within us. Bring to heart child prodigies, those with what seem to be extraordinary gifts. Such beings are attuned to frequencies of the Divine in such a way they are able to bring forth information that seems temporarily veiled from the rest.

Adventure with pleasing colors, sounds, scents and shapes. Gaze at crop circles.

You might find yourself aware of remarkable information and inner vistas.

Our Radiant Allowance

Did you receive an allowance when you were young?

Our allowance now is our Light to be here and to be happy.

We are Light and free!

When we help another to trust their inner felt sense of peace, and
when we care for everyone who is not feeling their Light (right)
to be, we deactivate our own existential sense of guilt and shame.

We feeeeeeel our radiant allowance!

In case you think there is not a sense of guilt within, inquire if you feel you
or others are guilty and deserve to be blamed or shamed for anything.

If you are truly free of any such thoughts and
feelings you are truly free. You are enlightened.

As we allow others their experience of playing in a realm of "you" and "me,"
we re-mind ourselves that we are profoundly cherished, beautiful and free.

Trust your radiant allowance and share it with everyOne.

We are peace. We are joy. We are Light.

Only Love and Light are Real

Have you ever had a dream that felt fearful? In the dream, you faced the fear and it dissolved? Divine Intelligence is sharing with us to hold to the Light in moments that feel dark or especially adventurous. As we apply peaceful practice to our "waking" lives, we witness the results during our days and during our nights. In this way, a transcendent space for miracles is opened. In fact, Jesus and A Course in Miracles are clear that, "Miracles are natural. They are our natural state. When they do not occur, something has gone wrong." What has gone wrong is that within our own mind we are choosing to trust fear, ego, our illusions, rather than Light's Loving eternal radiance. In choosing Love, especially when it feels hard and when others are involved, we may or may not see immediate shifts in our external world. Why? It may seem, from our perspective, to take time for quantum shifts to manifest in the physical realm. Shifts are actually instant. (Remember, form is dense. It is energy moving two times slower than the speed of light. We also do not presently have access to the Big Picture.) For now, there appear to be many individuals, all with free will and trajectories for our lives that are helpful. Never doubt, a real shift is occurring. The veils in our mind are dissolving. Look to the mass of stories in the world of people choosing Love and forgiveness (overlooking error) in challenging moments and how the quality of their lives improves and miracles flood.[66] As we face our internal fears while holding Love's hand everyone feels this on the quantum creative level because we are fundamentally joined as Divine Intelligence. Even in our deeply veiled state, we realize we are safe. As we know, there are many situations in this world where people forget to trust Love because we are so afraid to trust each other, let alone ourselves. Whether now or when our physical body passes away, what is real can be known if we are interested. We remain undiminished.

In Love, we find ourselves traveling toward OM.

---

66   Bring to heart stories of your own and in the lives of others when a safe, honoring space was held regardless of circumstances, stunning behaviors and internal fears.

Vibratory Thought Clearing

It is hard to miss from our Light adventuring
how vital it is to dismiss all thoughts of ego.

We know that deeply felt thought is creative.
At the quantum level, as we focus on fear and
step into bringing forth our ideas and beliefs in
separation, we bring about powerful alchemy.

Here is what the ancients taught:

Divine Intelligence wipes away thought-forms that
do not have enough energy within them to come forth.

This smoothing occurs during the dawn hours and the dusk,
a Divinely Intelligent transition zone between dark and light.

While shadow/ego will never be real, we can, as we are within,
manifest any dreamworld that we so desire...as a collective.

We can bring to heart any number of collective horror stories and
Love stories that, if we didn't believe in them when they were small,
could not have grown into bigger story. We wished them to be...to come.

Our adventure is that, because we are a unified awareness, if we are
"belief"ing in stories of separation, we create our own temporary hell.

Beings who undertake the Inner Journey come to realize this.
Remove mind from the matrix of false beliefs made manifest.

Those who choose to focus on the hellish will eventually come
to discover the mistake. We are not to force anyone to shift.
Indeed, we cannot force anyone to shift. This feeds shadow.
We cannot violate free will. All will awaken eventually.
All will realize that this is all a tiny, strange dreaming.

Look to any spirituality to learn of the dreaming.

Always Whole

We are not broken, nor have we ever been.

Have you believed messages to the contrary?

As Light, forgive the bearers of such communications.

The bearer has always been you. We are not guilty. Not ever.

Yet, we don't recall until we go within and Love what's round.

Messages of brokenness are misunderstandings of ancient wisdom.

We remain as were created,[67] perfect, whole and unspeakably cherished.

Remember, we are not our bodies. We are not our dreaming dramas.

We are Pure Awareness. We are radiant golden sun bow Light.

We are astonishing beyond our human mind's comprehension.

Research stories by those who share of our awareness.

Head outside. Breathe in the air. Gaze all around.

Ground into the earth's spherical mound.

Ground into the cosmic pulse of sound.

The sounds of the universe are a tiny blip of You.

---

67 Quote from *A Course in Miracles*, co-scribed by Dr. Schucman and Dr. Thetford, professors and medical psychologists working at Columbia University's College of Physicians and Surgeons (both deceased).

The Dream of Guns & Roses

Let's explore why there remains cruelty, hate and violence in our world:

We have partial amnesia of our origin. (Do you remember where you come from?)
The world is made from a thought to "be separate." This caused our fear and guilt.
We literally instantly felt alone and broken, not in words, but in a sensation.
Now, in our state, we cannot fully recall, unless we go deeply within,
that we are Divine Intelligence resting safely within perfection.
Light is now scary to us on an unconscious, existential level.
Light now seems quite a strange form of experience.

Yet, memory intact or slightly diminished, we remain as
we were created, Light, free, powerful co-creators.
Fundamentally One Singularity, a pure awareness.

Divine Intelligence always surrounds us. Always.

In the dreamtime, whatever we focus on we create.

Bring to mind all relations, peaceful and warlike, and all
material objects, pleasing or not pleasing, in the world.

They began as ideas. An idea of having a child.
An idea of building a fire, a tractor, a computer.

Our deeply felt ideas are in the collective dream field.

An idea of guns is in our collective dream field.
An idea of roses is in our collective dream field.

Everything is in our collective dream field. Every dream can also dissolve.
The more focus we place on Love and Light and that which reminds us of
our astonishingly wondrous nature (even if we don't believe in this at first!)
the more the unreal dissolves, and what has always been becomes clear.

This is reason enough to make every moment a smiling
adventure, most especially the unhappy feeling ones.

Awakening and Fear

While this has been stated before, it cannot be stated too often.

As we move toward awakening, our journey may feel more intense. This is not because our fear grows. This is because we are becoming more aware of the fear that is there that we had been denying. It only "feels" more intense. It is ancient and existential. It is vital to not buy into any stories in our mind that feel real, whether in waking or dreaming life, to help us overcome fear within our own mind. One who is very close to awakening may find his/herself experiencing what feels like innumerable tests. This is fear not Love.

We are undoing our wishing in our own mind. Ego wants to dream because it has forgotten it never really left peace and joy. It fights for its dreaming life. As more of us collectively focus on Love, we are causing awakening to be easier for everyone.

It is only our own ego/fear/shame that needs to be transcended.

Awakening has nothing to do with words, yet words are a tool. We are going for an undoing of our fear. As we pass through dark nights, trusting our Light through that which seems horrific and inescapable to our ego mind, we are activating our Light.

A modern teacher who, without sharing publicly what he was doing, helped millions of his readers open to higher awareness in a gentle manner. We all know C. S. Lewis, scholar, author and Christian apologetic, for his children's book series called The Narnia Chronicles. Dr. Lewis has a fascinating history. It has come to light that Lewis based the books on an ancient cosmology of the heavens,[68] what was referred to as the seven planets[69] of ancient times. While our present day cosmology looks quite different, there is esoteric and Christian mysticism associated with the cosmos that is stunning if one does the research. Planets and stars are considered to be living beings that serve and protect us during our awakening simply by what and where they are. Divine Intelligence knows what to place and where to place it. Always.

We are immersed within subtle and gross fields that affect everything. Indeed, our ego mind's opinion of Life is deeply limited. As we become more comfortable with feeeeeeeeeeeeeeling the Love inside, we are waking up.

---

68   *Planet Narnia* by Michael Ward, PhD.
69   The seven ancient planets were considered to be the Moon, the Sun, Mercury, Venus, Mars, Saturn and Jupiter. The Moon and the Sun were considered planets because, from the perspective of an earth dweller, they move around the heavens. The word "planet" in Greek means "wanderer."

Miracle Field

Not far from where I am living there is an athletic field called Miracle Field.
How cool is this? We are living within the field. We are at play in the field.

We are immersed within radiance.

Can you feel it, the miracle?

I can too. Absolutely.

It matters not our physical location or circumstances.
Trust Love's eternal, abiding, graceful presence.
Visualize a Golden Sun Bow of Radiance.
There has never been anything to fear.
We remain as we were created.
Only our mind is veiled to
our full radiance.
Extend Love
from your
Heart's
Core.

Ah.

Miracle Words

You already know I spend time with children.

We adventure with miracle words.

Two powerful ones are

The heartfelt, "Please"

and

The heartfelt, "Thank you"

Adventuring with miracle words helps remind our own mind that we are beautiful, wondrous, cherished, deeply wise and always helpful.

Create a list of your own miracle words.

The Language of Love is universal.

Words are only a start.

Thank you for all your kind words and works and play.

Give yourself a resounding round of applause!

Use your hands and your feet to clap!

Ego Needs a Hug

All of humanity has huge fears deep within the psyche.
Conditions within convey that something is being missed.

To ego, it seems counter intuitive to down right dangerous to uplift
someone who is acting out, yet this is exactly what we are being asked
by our Love to do. This message is everywhere, in all our literature,
spiritual and secular, taught by all our respected teachers. Most of all, this
knowingness of Love's presence is written in our hearts. How many times a
day do you and I walk away from conflict? Often. We are very wise.
Ego's drama is the same whether from a child or a grown-up in any arena of life.

Forgive the dream drama and the dreamer.

Ego is afraid to trust peace. Our heart is not.
Only you can make the choice to go within.

This is our free will. To know our Light or to forget our Light.

We can continue to trust our fear, or we can make another choice.
We are not judged for our fear and for our resistance to trusting
Love. This is important. Give yourself and everyone an existential
hug. We are often afraid, especially when we don't know it.

When I feel afraid, I look toward those who have said YES! to Love in dark
feeling circumstances. We can bring to mind many. They are you and me.
There is no "other." We are One. "They" is a myth we brought into being.

Love you and trust that everyone of us is doing our very best.

Here are some glorious films that demonstrate awakening.

A Beautiful Mind
Seven Years in Tibet
Peaceful Warrior
Spider Man
Leap Year
Shark Boy and Lava Girl

Our Species and Divine Intelligence

In the truest sense, we need not fear.[70]

When we trust the beliefs and vibrations of fear
we manifest the fearful. This is natural resonance.
This is quantum physics. A Law of Divine Intelligence.

All we need to do is trust Love's Presence and overlook our fear.
In this way, we naturally become kinder and wiser toward all Life.
Awakening for us all comes naturally by trusting Divine Intelligence.

The veils in our mind vanish when we trust Love
whether or not our mind recognizes this effect.

Some children are aware this world is a dream.
I am aware that the world isn't my home.
Your heart is aware that you dream.
Yet, we are meant to enjoy this!

Act Lovingly and Go Within.
You will remember the Truth.
Share distress with the Light.
We are Divine Intelligence.
We are the Light of One.

We are waking up to wondrous Life.

May we finish our dream in grace
and return to our paradise place.

Thank you for existing!

---

70   *There is nothing to fear* is a key teaching. Trusting our fear and not forgiving self and others reinforces a false state of mind that creates illusion/suffering. It is quite the adventure to transcend all fear in the veiled state, so trust and have faith that all is well when you are not feeling at peace and in joy. Trust stillness.

Thank you for Exploring *The Mix Up* and for Adventuring in this World

Two nights ago I had a dream of a man with a box for a head. There was a shut metal door where a face would normally be. In the next moment the heavy door was open. The face I could now see was made of grey metal, like pewter. The eyes were closed, yet peaceful. Each time we choose love over the fear in our mind, we are opening a door that transcends ego. Each time we extend a loving thought, our heart remembers.

Smile with every particle of your being.

Trust that everything is perfect,

though this may see not right.

Only Love's Light is real.

~ ~ ~

Ignite your faithful heart.

Pomp and Circumstance

Can you feel the heavenly celebrations?

The waving of the Inner Light?

The One Team is worth playing for.

Our existence is a miracle.

Love with all your might.

Trust your Light.
Forgive the world.
Bless the world.

If you grow weary, just remember well,
traveling Light we always have friends.

We are as One.

Wondrous Resources

(The best resource is within you. Locate resources that Light up your Inner Joy.)

Here are a few of my own favorites:

A Course in Miracles
Co-scribed by Dr. Helen Schuchman and Dr. William Thetford

Psychotherapy: Purpose, Process and Practice
Co-scribed by Dr. Helen Schuchman and Dr. William Thetford

The Song of Prayer
Co-scribed by Dr. Helen Schuchman and Dr. William Thetford

Holy Spirit's Interpretation of the New Testament
Scribed by Regina Dawn Akers

The Story of Edgar Cayce: There is a River
Thomas Sugrue

Never Forget to Laugh: A Biography of Dr. William Thetford
Dr. Thetford is co-scribe of A Course in Miracles.
Author Carol Howe was a long-time friend of Bill's.

The Jeshua Letters
Jon Marc Hammer

Medicine Cards
Jamie Sams and David Carson

The Divine Matrix
Gregg Braden

Stalking the Wild Pendulum: On the Mechanics of Consciousness
Itzak Bentov, Biomedical Scientist and Mystic

HeartMath.com

Trust the Infinitely Radiant You.

About the Author

Laura Bedford is a gentle, playful teacher of peace. She assists youth and adults to realize we have all we need within and free their mind of ego's guilt, shame and fear, the only blocks to the awareness of our Inner Light. As we trust our own and everyone's beauty, wholeness and Light, we enlighten to our True Radiant Nature.

As a child, Laura had an on-going mystical experience that helped her trust her inner knowing. Throughout her life, she has continued to experience expanded states of awareness, visions and "the impossible." Deeply aware of the fact that only Love is real, and unkindness, suffering and not remembering how she came to be in this world was not natural, in 1992, Laura began formal studies into God. She now speaks fluently on guilt/ego-mind and Divine Awareness. She shares in gentle, deeply poignant ways with youth and adults on the existence of the Inner Light and why it makes all the difference (quickens our ability to transcend guilt) when we affirm everyone's Light, beauty and wholeness and trust our joy and Love to awaken.

For more information, visit
trustingourinnerlight.org or **radiantkids.com**

Laura is available for speaking engagements.

Made in the USA
Charleston, SC
16 April 2015